Right@Sight
Grade 1

Based on
Read and Play
(original and new series) by
T. A. Johnson

Revised by Caroline Evans

With additional material by Paul Terry

Frankfurt/M • Leipzig • London • New York

Peters Edition Limited
2–6 Baches Street
London
N1 6DN

First published 2001
© 2001 by Peters Edition Limited, London

All rights reserved. No part of this publication may be reproduced, stored in a retrieval system or transmitted in any form or by any means, electronic, mechanical, photocopying, recording or otherwise, without the prior written permission of the publisher.

Music-setting and typesetting by Musonix

Cover design by Nick Wakelin
Cover layout and typography by adamhaydesign.com
Text design by c eye, London
Printed in Great Britain by Halstan & Co,
Amersham, Bucks.

Set in Monotype Garamond 3 and Frutiger

Right@Sight
Grade 1

A note to teachers

Sight-reading is one of the most important skills for any musician, and certainly not to be seen as a chore necessary only for passing exams! Right@Sight will help to develop and improve that skill, providing a structured approach and opportunities for regular practice. Hints are provided for the earlier pieces to focus attention on notation, form, texture, interpretation and technique, prompted with questions (left-hand column) and information (right). These should also help to encourage greater musical awareness in all of a student's performing.

In an examination, half a minute will be given to prepare the sight-reading, and the examiner is likely to remind candidates that they may play the music during this time. Encourage your students to try out the opening, the ending and any awkward-looking passages so that they are well prepared before the test starts. Instil careful attention to the fundamental elements of Time, Rhythm and Key – though the key signature comes first on the staff, it is often the first piece of information to be forgotten in performance!

Becoming a good sight-reader needs daily practice, and regular 'exercise' with Right@Sight will prepare students to tackle whatever music they may want to play. Towards the end of the section with commentary, some pieces go a little beyond the standard expected for the grade, so as to stretch players' ability and enable them to face any sight-reading test with increased confidence: to play it right – at sight!

Caroline Evans

Key to symbols

1	Exercise number
T	Time
R	Rhythm
K	Key
?	Questions
!	Watch out

Contents

Section 1:	Focusing on the keys of C major, G major and F major	4
Section 2:	Introducing quavers	7
Section 3:	Introducing staccato playing	15
Section 4:	Introducing the rhythm: ♩. ♪	17
Section 5:	Introducing the key of D major and the time signatures of 2/2 and 3/8	21
Section 6:	Introducing tied notes	23
Section 7:	Introducing accidentals and the keys of A minor and D minor	27
Section 8:	On your own now …	31
Section 9:	Glossary of musical terms and symbols	40

Right@Sight

Focusing on the keys of C major, G major and F major

1 Follow the **TRaK**

- **T** What does the time signature tell you?   There are ..... **crotchet** beats in a bar.
- **R** Can you clap the rhythm?   Count while clapping.
- **K** What is the key?   Play the broken chords in bars 1 and 5.
- **?** How many beats are there in a dotted minim?   There is a dotted minim in bars 4 and 8.
- **!** **Watch out** for the interval of a third in bar 7.

Place both hands on the keyboard, then play through with confidence and a good tone.
Try not to look at the keyboard and keep your eyes on the music.

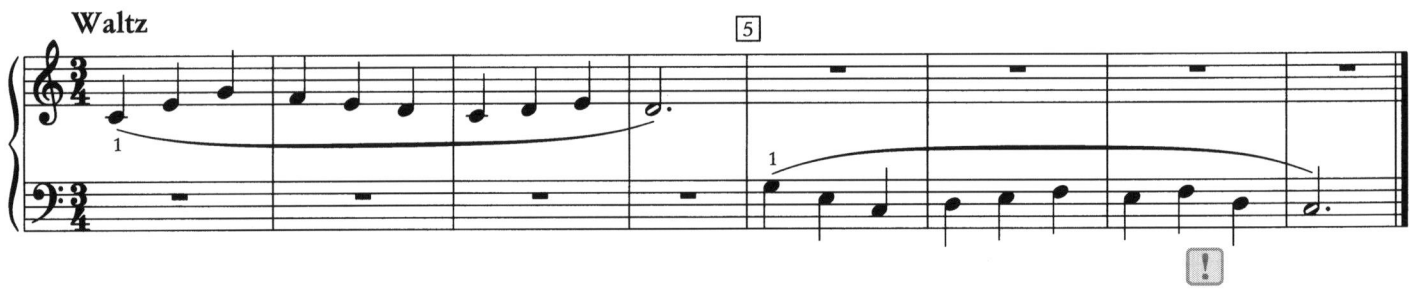

2
- **T** How many beats are there in a bar?   Note the value of each beat.
- **R** Can you clap or tap the rhythm?   Keep counting as you clap or tap.
- **K** What is the key?   Find and name the broken chord in bar 3.
- **?** How many beats are the notes worth in bars 4 and 8?   A complete bar's rest is shown in the same way as a semibreve rest.
- **!** **Watch out** for the repeated notes in bar 1, and the intervals of a third in bars 3 and 6.

Place the finger you will need on the first note in bar 1 (right hand) and on the first note in bar 5 (left hand).
Play through the piece steadily without stopping.

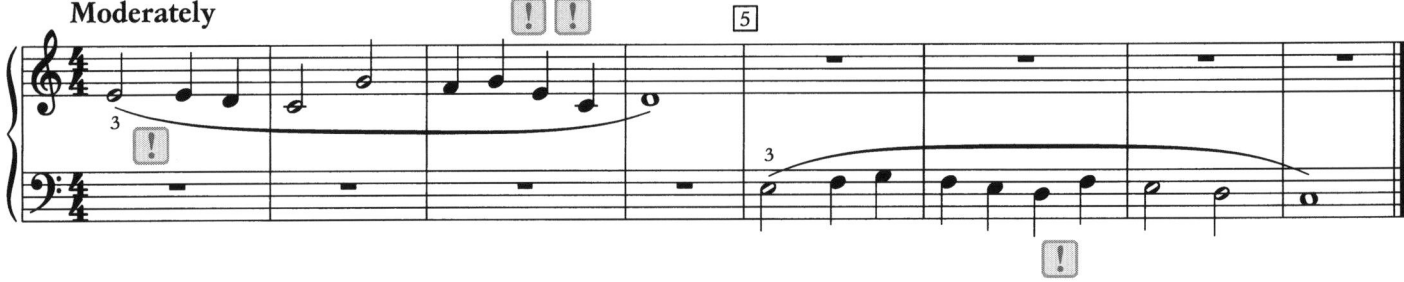

T	What does the time signature tell you?	The lower number in the time signature indicates the kind of beat it is.
R	Can you tap the rhythm?	Keep counting as you clap or tap.
K	What is the key? How many F♯s are there?	Find the broken chord.
?	What kind of rest appears in bar 4 (right hand)?	Don't forget to lift the hand where the rest occurs.

Place the finger you will need on the first note in bar 1 (right hand) and on the first note in bar 5 (left hand). Have your 3rd finger ready over the black key in the bass clef. Play through firmly and steadily.

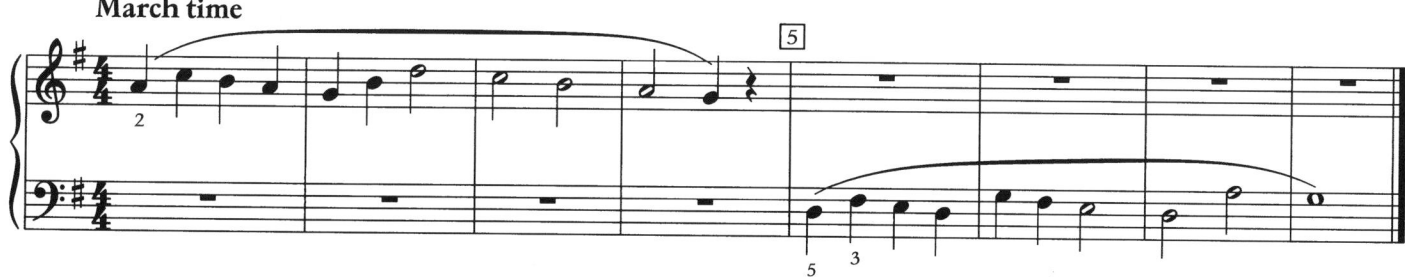

T	What does the time signature tell you?	The value of each beat is a ....
R	Can you tap the rhythm?	There are two crotchet rests in this piece.
	Is the **rhythm** the same in both hands?	Now compare the **melody** in bars 1–4 with bars 5–8.
K	What is the key?	Find all the B♭s in this piece.
?	How many beats are there in a minim?	There is a minim in bars 4 and 8.

Begin the piece quite loudly, then play quietly at the end.

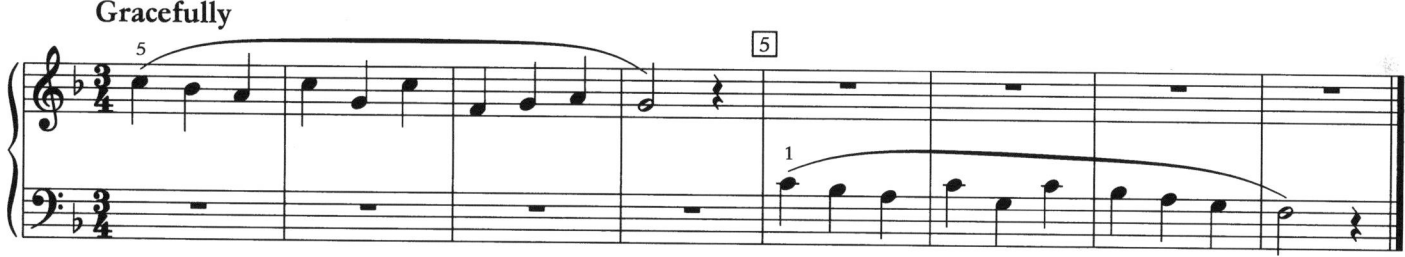

T	Is this in duple, triple or quadruple (2, 3 or 4) time?	There are .... beats in a bar.
R	Can you tap the rhythm?	Notice that the rhythm is the same in both hands.
K	Can you play the key (or tonic) chord?	The melody moves mainly by step.

Play through gracefully without stopping. Keep your eyes on the music and try not to look at your hands.

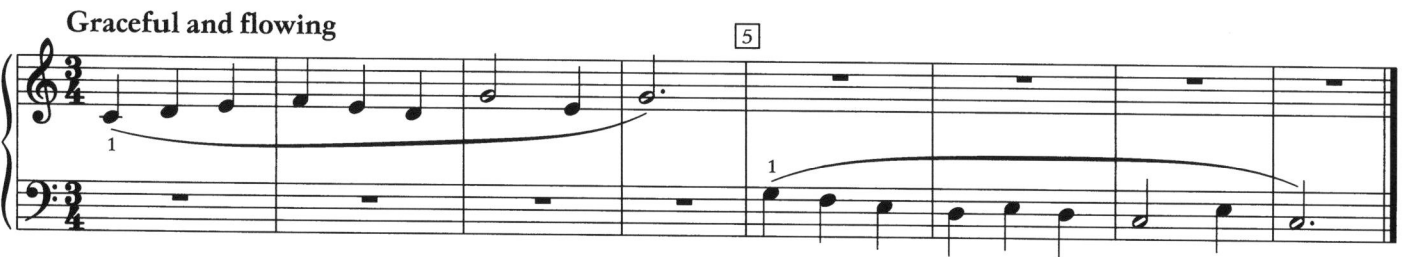

6

[T] How many beats are there in a bar?

[R] Can you tap the rhythm: right hand on your right knee, left hand on your left knee?

[K] What is the key?

[?] Can you find an interval of a fourth?

The value of each beat is a crotchet.

Notice that the rhythm in bars 7 and 8 is different from that in bars 4 and 5.

Give the minims their correct value.

Notice the shape of the melody.

Play this piece with confidence and a good firm tone.

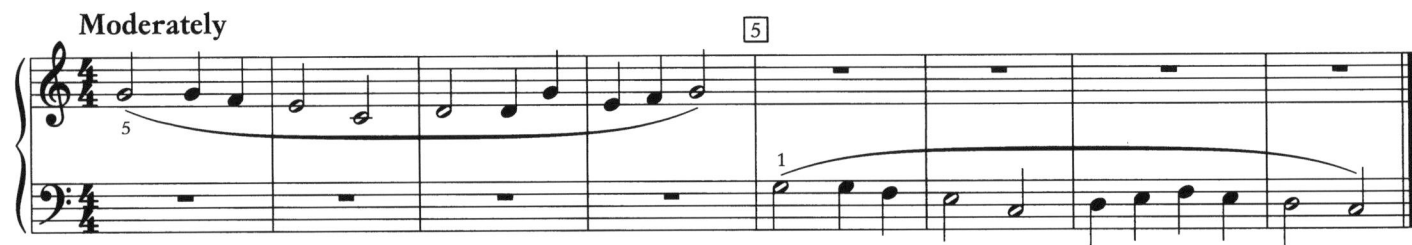

7

[T] Is this duple, triple or quadruple time?

[R] Can you tap the rhythm?

[K] Can you name the key?

[?] How many beats are there in the semibreves?

Give the value of the beat.

Notice that the rhythm is the same in both hands.

Play the key (or tonic) chord.

Hold the minims for their correct value.

Place your hands over the keys with the correct fingers ready for each note. Play firmly and steadily, like a march.

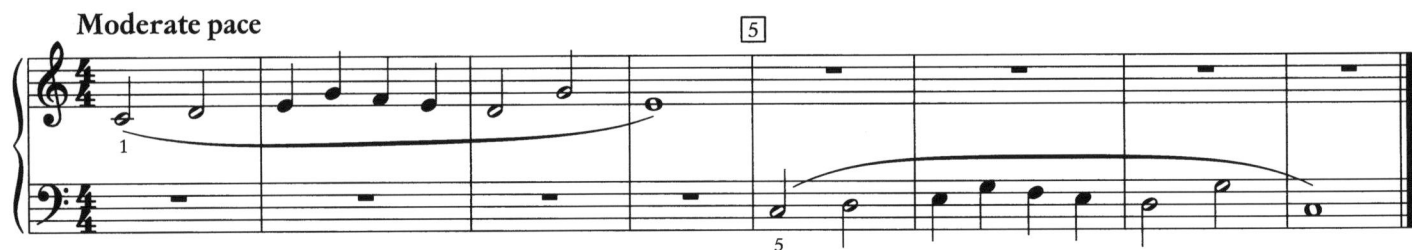

8

Follow the [TRaK]

[R] Can you tap the rhythm?

[?] Can you find the interval of a fifth and two intervals of a third?

Here is another piece in C major.

Notice that the rhythm is the same in both hands.

Look at the pattern of the melody and see how it moves mainly by step.

Play this majestically and loudly. Keep your eyes on the music and try not to look down at the keyboard.

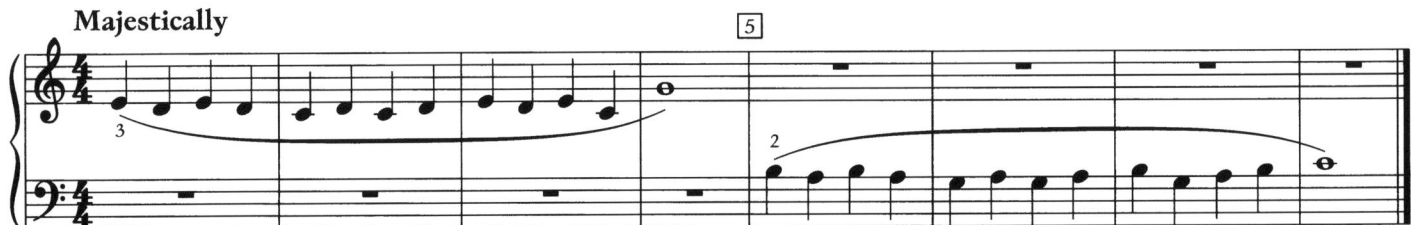

Right@Sight

Introducing quavers

[T] How many beats are there in a bar?
[R] Can you tap the rhythm?

The beats are crotchets.
There are ..... quavers in a crotchet.
Practise tapping crotchets in the right hand and quavers in the left hand. Then swap over.

[?] What is the key?

Play the key (or tonic) chord.

[!] **Watch out** for the crotchet E in bar 2 (left hand) and bar 6 (right hand).

Make sure the quavers are correctly timed. Count while playing the piece through.

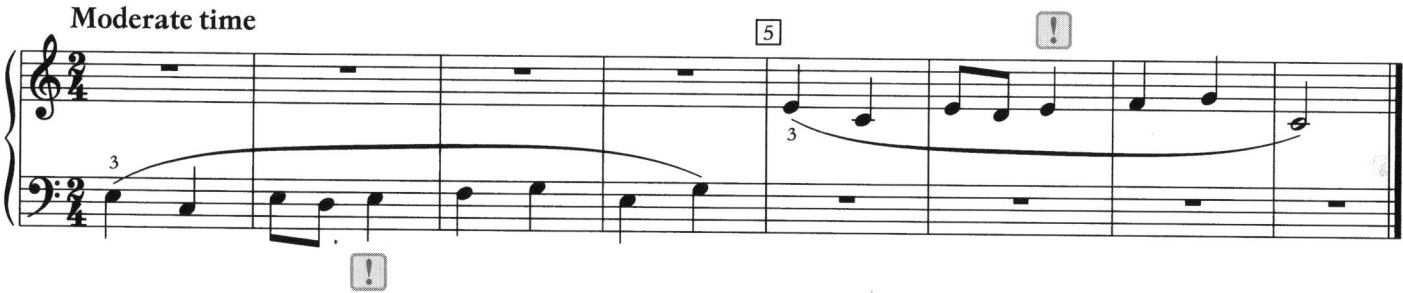

[T] What is the time signature?
[R] Can you tap the rhythm?

The value of each beat is a ....
Count as you tap, keeping the quavers even. Remember to count two beats for the minims.

[K] What is the key?
Are any of the notes affected by the sharp?

Play the key-note (or tonic).

Play boldly without stopping.

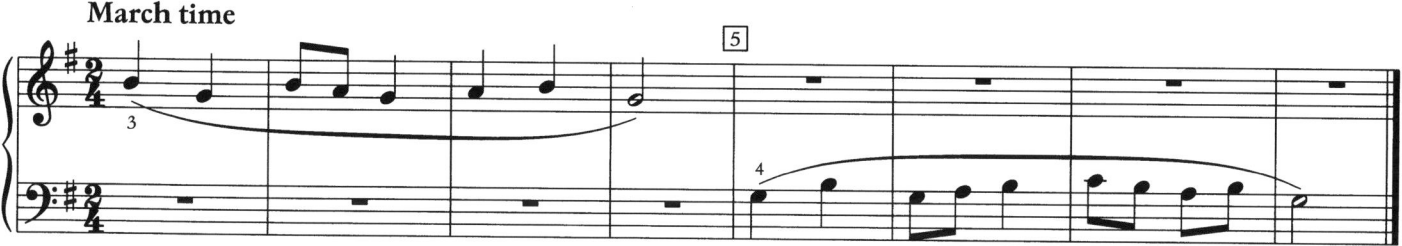

11
- [T] How many beats are there in a bar?
- [R] Can you tap the rhythm?
- [K] Are there any B♭s?
- [!] **Watch out** for the repeated notes in bars 1 and 3.

A march is always in 2 or 4 time.
State the value of the rest in bar 4 (left hand).
Find all the notes affected by the flat.

Let the quavers run up and down very neatly and smoothly (*legato*).

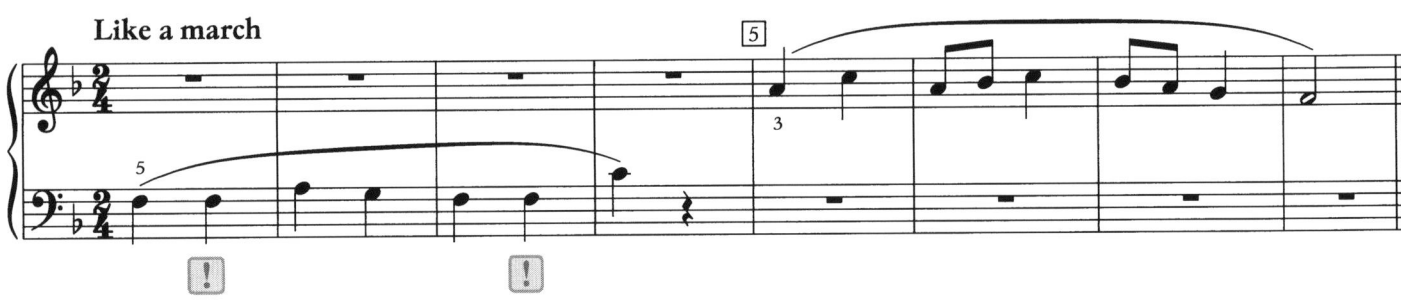

12
- [T] Is this in duple, triple or quadruple time?
- [R] Can you tap the rhythm?
- [K] What is the key?
- [!] **Watch out** for the interval of a fourth in bar 4.

A waltz is a dance in three time.
Remember to give the minims their full value.
See if there are any notes affected by the sharp.

Place the correct finger on the first note of bar 1 and on the first note of bar 5. Count the beats aloud as you play.

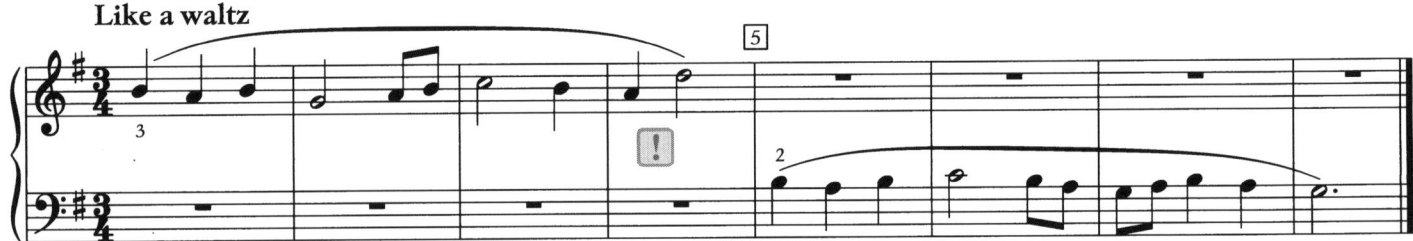

13
- [T] What is the time signature?
- [R] Can you tap the rhythm: right hand on the right knee and left hand on the left knee?
- [K] What does the key signature tell you?

Here is another waltz.

Try and keep the quavers very even and smooth (*legato*). Count 3 beats on the dotted minims.

Notice the broken chord of G major in bar 1 and the little scale passage in bar 3.

Have the correct finger ready for the first note in bar 5 before you begin to play.
This is a fairly quiet piece (*mezzo piano*). Try not to look at your hands.

Follow the TRaK

[?] How many B♭s are there in the left hand?

What do you notice when you compare the two phrases?

Play the black key required for this piece.

The long curved lines above the notes are called phrase marks.

14

Remember to place **both** hands on the keyboard before you play. Try to keep your eyes on the bar ahead of the one you are playing. Play this piece in a lively and cheerful (*Allegro*) manner.

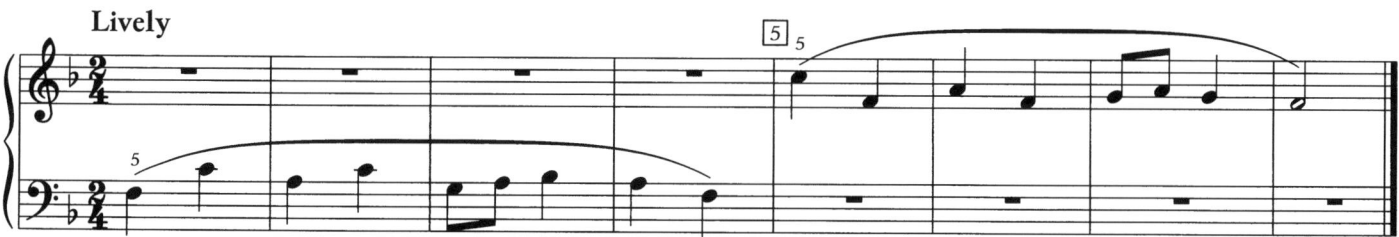

TRaK

[?] Which bars contain quavers?

What are the differences between the two phrases?

Look at the time signature; clap the rhythm; and name the key.

Make sure that the quavers are correctly timed. Also give the minims and semibreves their full value.

Notice the intervals of a third and the descending pattern of the melody.

15

First place both hands over the keys and then play in a quick and lively (*Allegro*) manner. Keep counting.

TRaK

[?] Is the time duple, triple or quadruple?

Do you notice the scale passages?

[!] **Watch out** for the quavers in bar 7.

This is a march. Count steadily.

Compare the two phrases.

16

Play the whole piece very smoothly (*legato*) with a good firm tone.

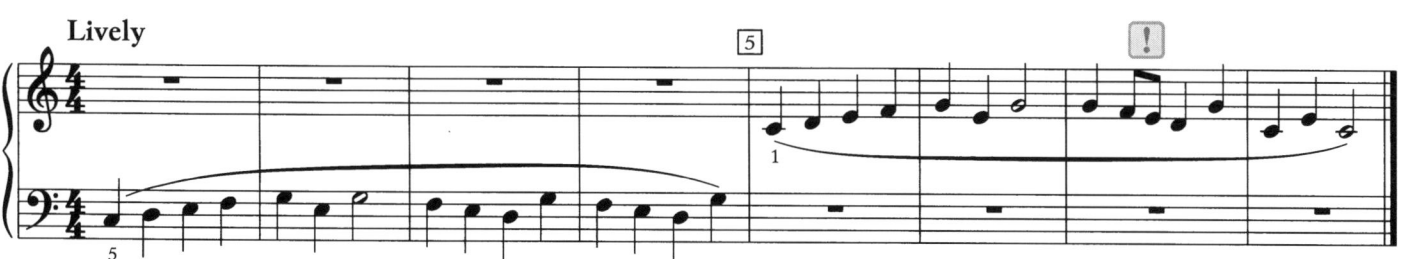

17

- **T** What does the time signature tell you? — A minuet is a dance in triple time.
- **R** Can you tap the rhythm? — Count as you tap.
- **K** What is the key? — Find all the notes to be flattened.
- **?** Can you name the broken chords in bars 1 and 5? — Play them as block chords.
- What do you notice when you compare the two phrases? — Make a note of the crotchet rests.

This piece should be played in a stately manner. Play without stopping or looking at the keyboard.

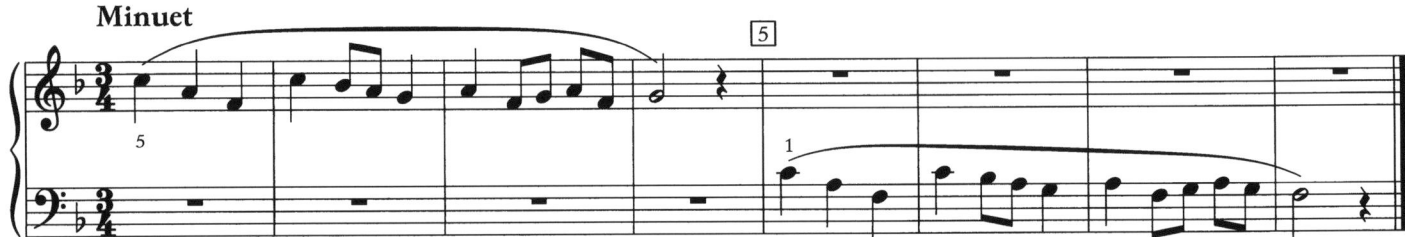

18

- Follow the **TRaK** — Find all the notes to be lowered a semitone.
- **?** What is the value of the dot in the dotted minims? — Give the dotted minims their full value.
- What do you notice when you compare the two phrases? — Look at the shape of the melody and see how it moves downwards mainly by step.
- **!** **Watch out** for the interval of a third in bar 7.

Play very smoothly and gracefully. Look ahead. After playing to the end, play bars 1–4 again, then try singing them.

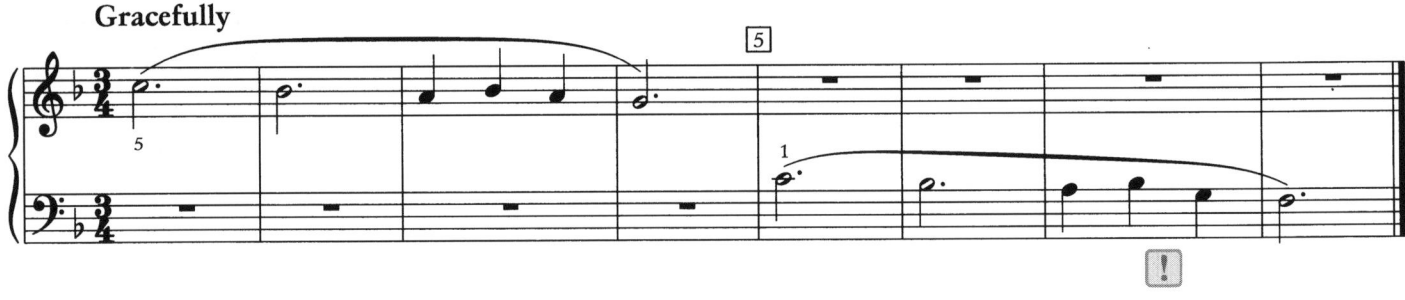

19

- **T**ime, **R**hythm and **K**ey
- **?** What (major) key does the key signature suggest? — Find any broken chords and play them as block chords.

Count as you play. Always look ahead.
Play the first two bars again and then sing them as an echo. Do the same with the next two bars.

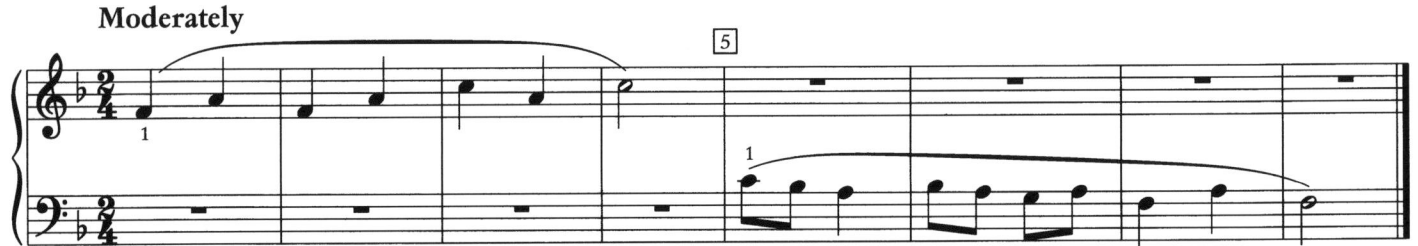

TRaK

? Which is quieter, *mp* or *p*?

! **Watch out** for the minims in bars 2 and 4.

Play the tonic chord. Is the F♯ used in this piece?

The full Italian term for *mp* is *mezzo piano*.

20

Place both hands ready over the keys before you begin. Play gracefully (*grazioso*) and smoothly (*legato*).
Try to keep your eyes on the bar ahead of the one you are playing.

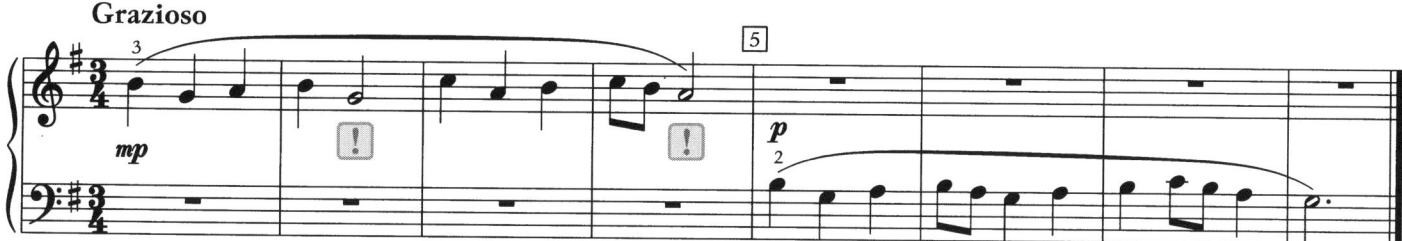

Time, **R**hythm and **K**ey?

? Are there any intervals of a third?

What do you notice about the shape of the melody?

! **Watch out** for the semibreves in bars 1 and 5.

Play the key-note.

Name the intervals in bar 8.

Notice how the melody moves mostly in steps.

21

Play loudly (*forte*) and with confidence.
Afterwards play the right hand again two bars at a time and try singing the melody as an echo.

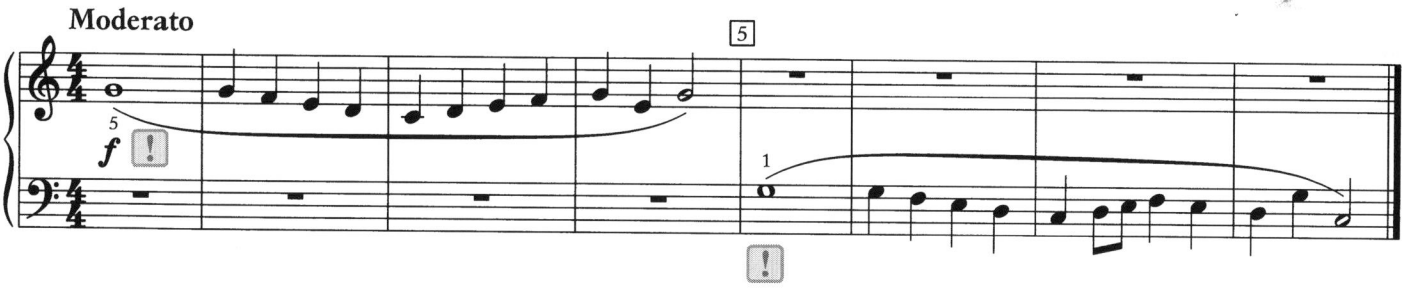

TRaK

Time all the quavers exactly; tap the rhythm;
and find all the flats.

22

This is a quick and lively piece (*Allegro*). The first phrase is quiet (*piano*); the second phrase is loud (*forte*).
Keep counting and keep going!

11

23

[TRaK]

[?] What does *mf* mean?

Play the tonic chord and find how many notes are affected by the flat in the key signature.

Give the meaning of *mp*.

There are several quaver groups in this piece. Count carefully.
Place both hands in position over the keys before you begin and then play in a fairly quickly (*Allegretto*).

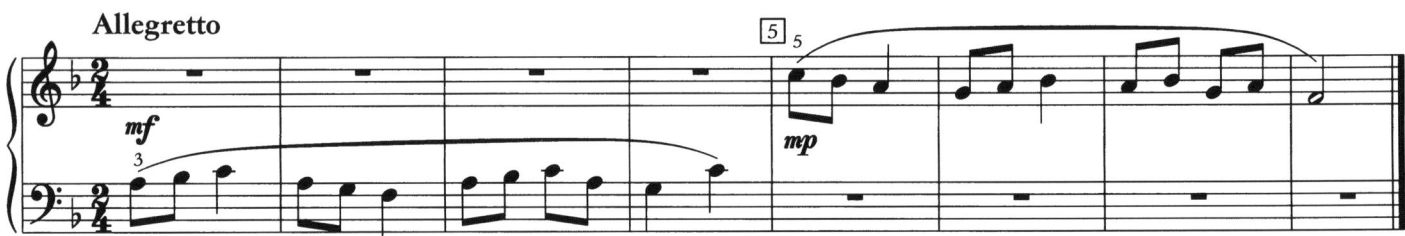

24

[T] What is the time signature?

[R] Can you tap the rhythm: left hand on the left knee, right hand on the right knee?

[K] Can you find the key-note? – without looking!

[!] **Watch out** for the repeated note in bar 3.

Another name for this is Common Time.

Make sure that the dotted minims are held for their full value.

(Feel for the pattern of the black notes.)

Place your hands over the notes with the correct fingers ready to play.
Keep the phrases as smooth (*legato*) as possible.

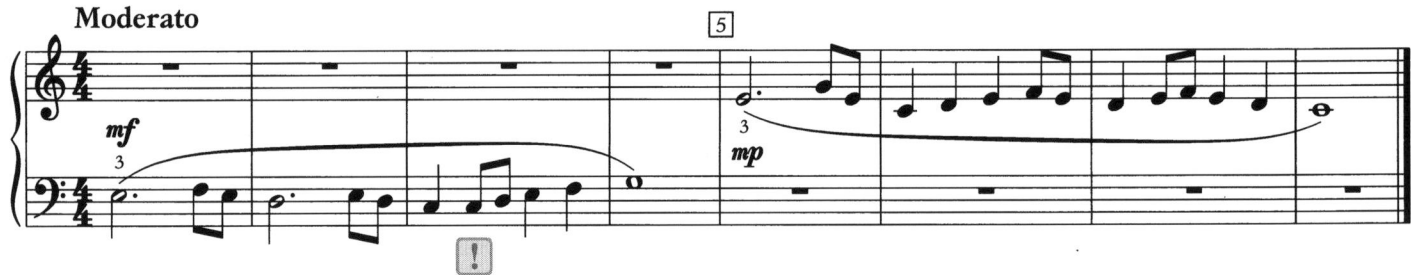

25

[TRaK]

[?] Can you name and play the broken chord in bars 1 to 2?

[!] **Watch out** for the crotchet rests in bar 4 (left hand) and bar 8 (right hand).

Note the dotted minims.

There is an interval of a .... in bar 5.

Don't forget to tap the rhythm first and then play with a good, firm tone in a marching style.

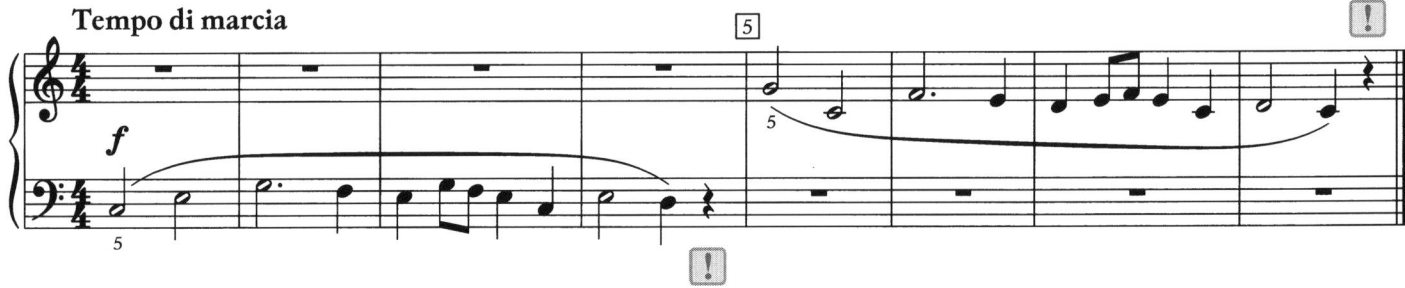

[T] What does the time signature tell you?   This is simple triple time.
[R] Can you tap the rhythm?   Count aloud as you tap the rhythm.
[K] What is the flat in the key signature?   Find all the notes to be played on a black key.
[!] **Watch out** for bars 2, 4 and 6, where the crotchet is followed by a minim. The fingering also needs care.

Count while playing this through slowly (*Adagio*).

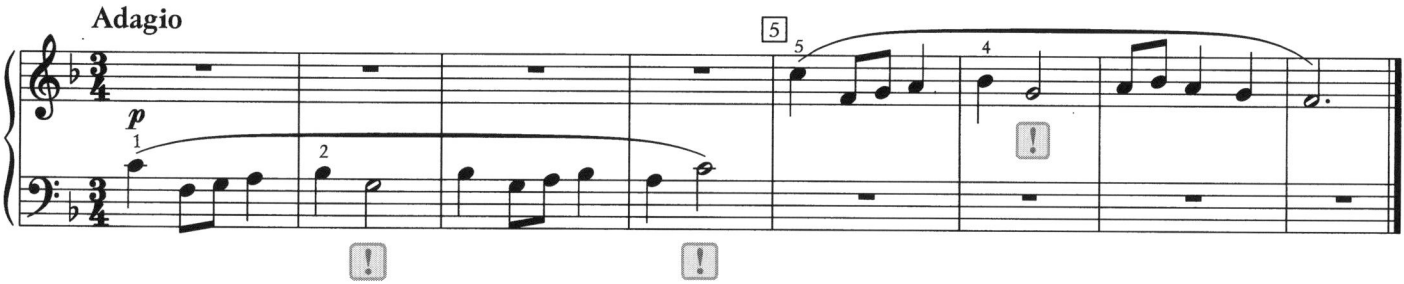

[TRaK]   Play the key-note or tonic.
[?] How many beats are there in a dotted minim?   Count aloud while tapping the rhythm.
[!] **Watch out** for the repeated notes in bars 1 and 2; and the crotchet rest in bar 4.

Play rhythmically in the style of a march. Look ahead.

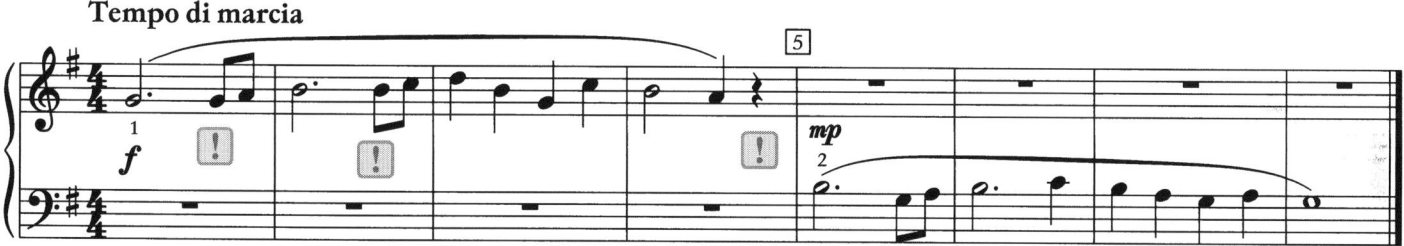

[TRaK]   Note the scale passages in bars 1 and 5.
[?] Can you find all the intervals of a third?   Compare the first two bars with bars 5 and 6. They are the same but in different octaves.

Which is quieter, **mp** or **mf**?   Note the crescendo sign ⎯⎯⎯⎯ towards the end.

Move this piece along (*con moto*) in a lively manner taking care to play the quaver passages very evenly.

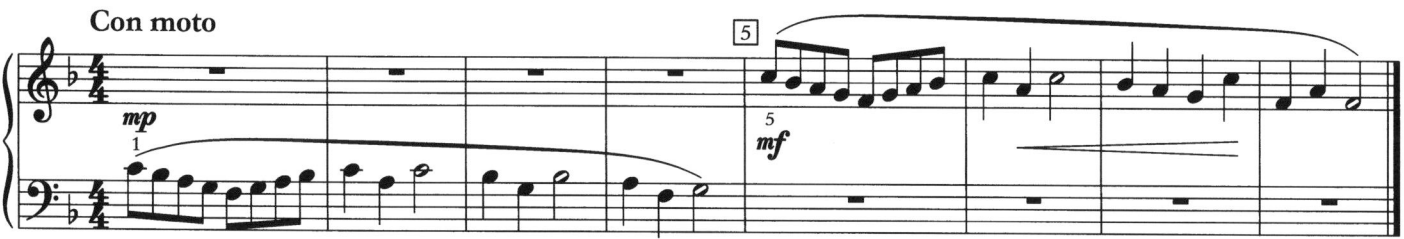

29

[TRaK]

[?] What are the curved lines beneath the notes?

Do you notice how the dynamics (*f*, *pp*) change?

[!] **Watch out** for the interval of a third in bar 7.

There are more quaver groups in this piece.

Lift your hand neatly at the end of each slur.

The sign at the end means ....

Play very rhythmically and brightly.

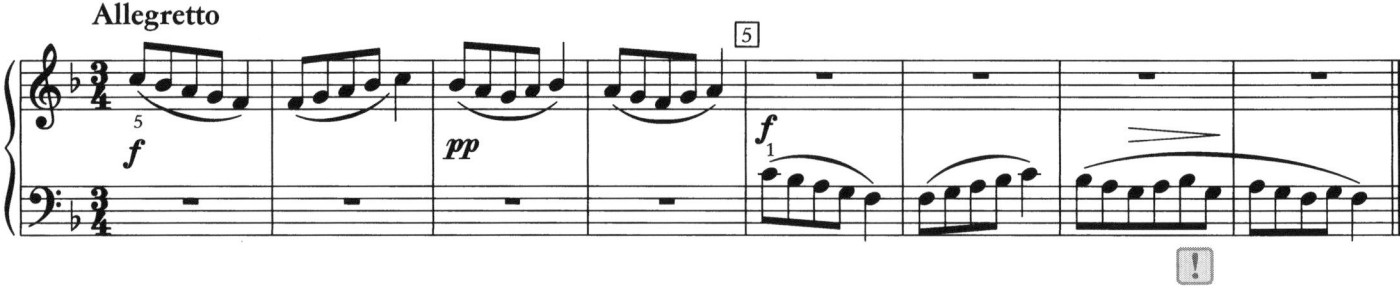

30

[T] Is the piece in duple, triple or quadruple time?

[R] Can you count as you tap the rhythm?

[K] What is the key?

[?] What do you notice when you compare bars 1 to 4 and bars 5 to 8?

Can you observe the phrasing?

Give the minims and semibreves their full value.

Find the notes to be played on a black key.

Raise the hand slightly at the end of each slur.

Place your fingers in the correct position over the keys. Then play gracefully.

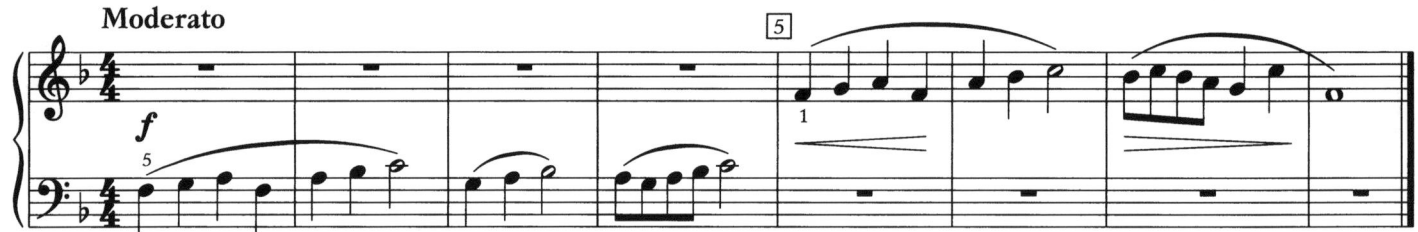

31

[T] Is the time duple, triple or quadruple?

[R]

[K] Are there any notes to be played on a black key?

[?] What is the meaning of *rit.*?

Give the value of the beat.

Tap the rhythm, timing the quavers evenly.

Play the tonic chord.

Note the 'extra' bar, or coda, at the end of the piece.

Play rhythmically and firmly.

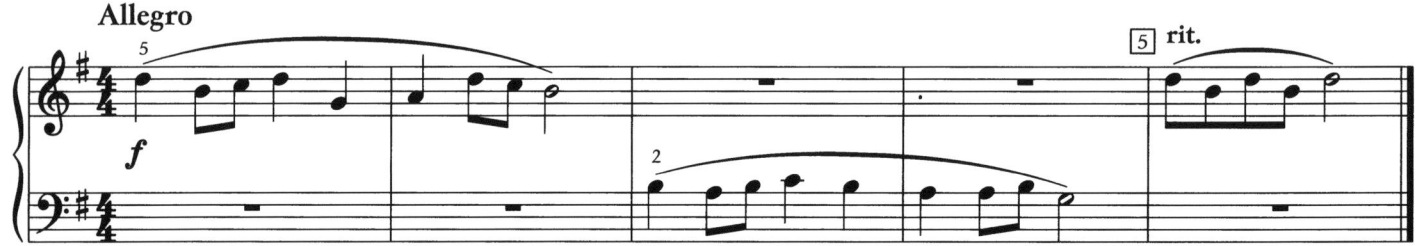

Right@Sight

Introducing staccato playing

TRaK 32

? Which notes are to be played *staccato*?

! **Watch out** for the repeated Gs in bars 1, 2, 5 and 6 – and the intervals of a third in bar 7.

Look at the time signature; tap the rhythm; name the key. This is a march.

Staccato means detached. Just raise your wrist and finger slightly when playing.

Play steadily and loudly (*forte*). Try not to allow a loud tone to become harsh.

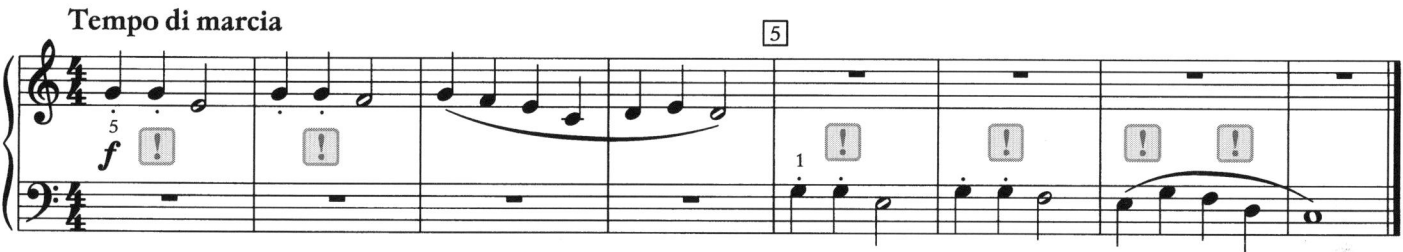

TRaK 33

? Are there any broken chords?

! **Watch out** for the slurs and *staccato* notes in every bar. Practise all these separately with the correct fingers, on the lid of the piano, before you play.

This is in triple time – a waltz. Find all the B♭s.

Find the intervals of a third. There is also a fourth.

TRaK 34

! **Watch out** for the slurred couplets in bars 1, 2, 5 and 6.

Give the dotted minim in bar 8 its full value.

Remember to tap the rhythm.
Have your fingers ready over the notes and then play slowly (*Adagio*) and quietly (*piano*).

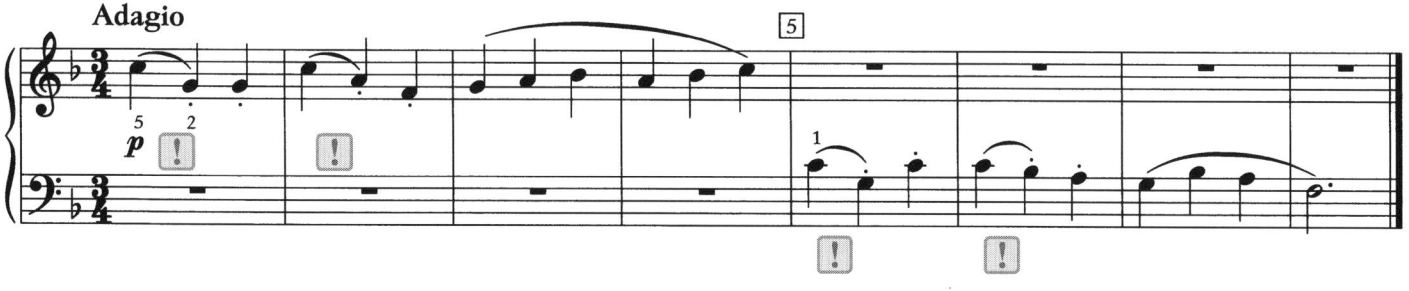

35

- **T** What does the time signature tell you?
- **R** Can you count as you tap the rhythm?
- **K** What is the key?   Find the notes to be flattened.

This little piece should be performed with confidence. Play the *staccato* notes crisply in contrast to the slurred notes.

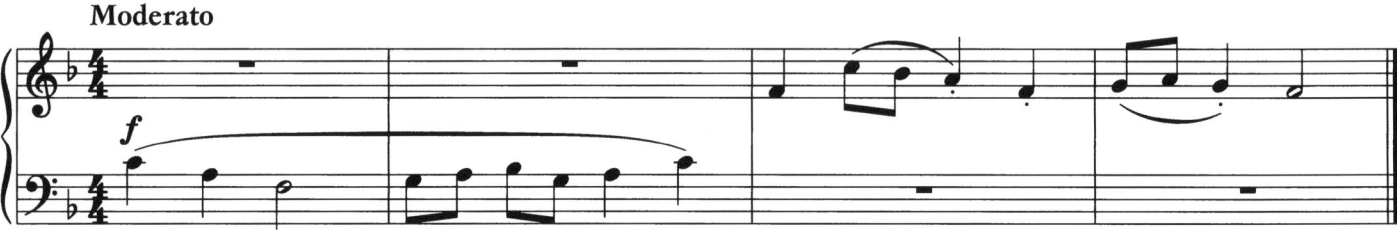

36

- **T** How many beats are there in a bar?
- **R** Can you tap the rhythm: right hand on your   Look for any *staccato* notes as you tap.
  right knee, left hand on your left knee?
- **K** What is the sharp in the key signature?   Name the key.
- **!** **Watch out** for the repeated notes in bars 2 and 5 particularly.

This lively piece should be played boldly at the beginning, becoming gradually slower and quieter (*rit. e dim.*) in the final bars.

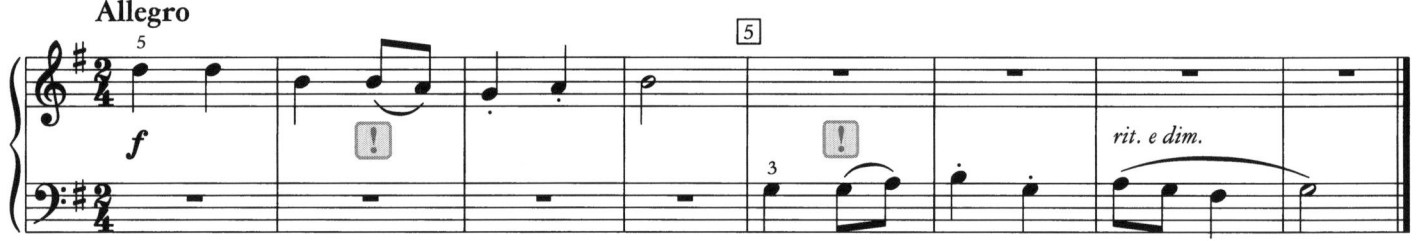

37

TRaK

- **?** What do you notice when you compare bars 1   Observe the crotchet rests in bars 2 and 5.
  and 2 (right hand) with bars 3 and 4 (left hand)?
  Is there a coda ('extra' phrase at the end of the piece)?   Give the meaning of *staccato*.
- **!** **Watch out** for the interval of a third in the group of quavers in bars 2 and 4.

Play this piece decisively, in a military style.

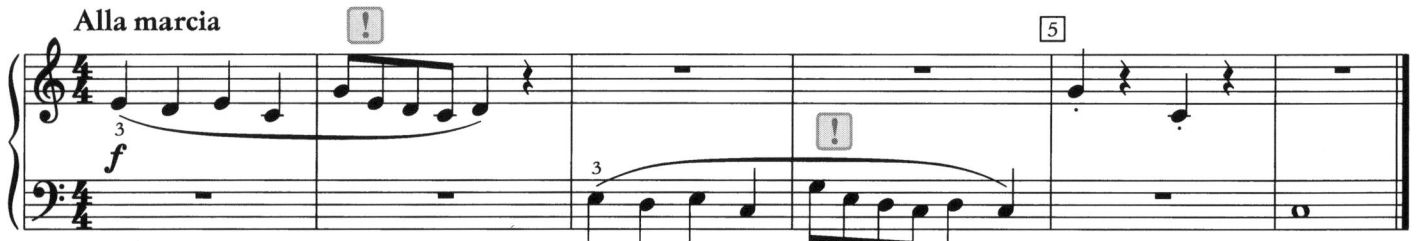

Right@Sight

Introducing the rhythm: ♩. ♪

T	What is the time signature?
R	What is the rhythm?

Note the value of each beat.

Clap this rhythm a few times and count while clapping:

Note the value of the dot.

K	What is the key?
?	Can you plan the fingering yourself?
!	**Watch out** for the dotted crotchet followed by a quaver in bars 1 and 3.

In this piece none of the notes is affected by the sharp.

Play through with confidence and a good tone.

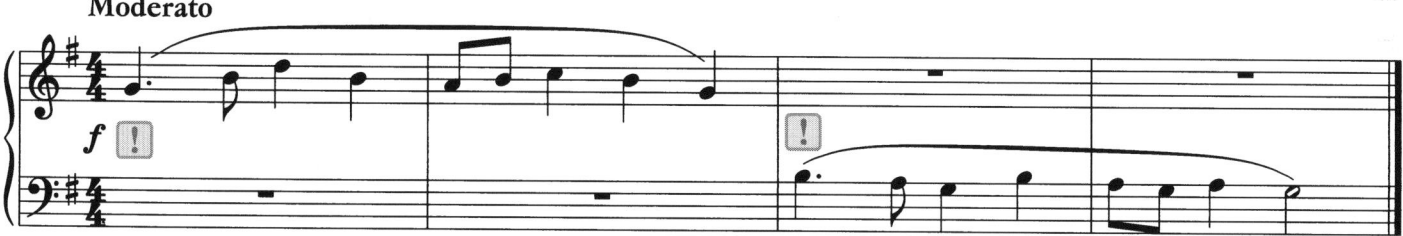

38

Follow the TRaK

? What is the value of the dot?

The timing of the dotted crotchet followed by a quaver needs care.

Tap the bars containing the dotted note several times while counting:

Can you find an interval of a third?

Can **you** plan the fingering?

Notice that the melody moves mostly by step.

Remember to place both hands over the keys so that the left hand is ready to play on time.

Play through smoothly (*legato*).

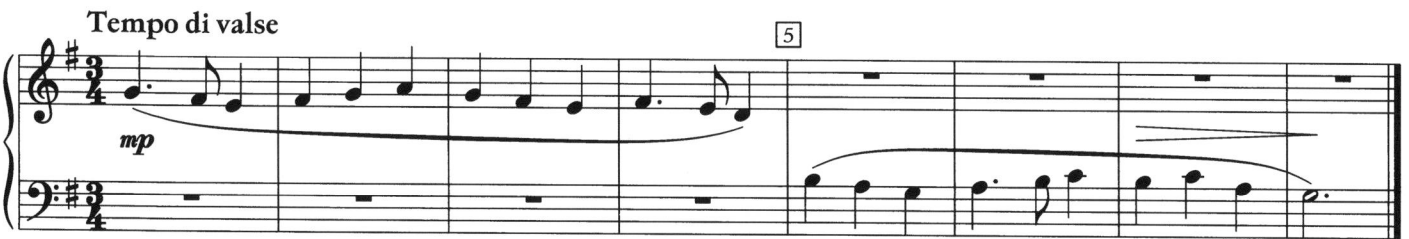

39

40

TRaK

? What do you notice when you compare the two phrases?

Name the major key that has F# in the key signature.

Notice that part of the scale appears in the last two bars.

! **Watch out** for the dotted crotchet followed by a quaver in bars 1 and 5.

Place the fingers ready over the keys. Keep counting as you play steadily.

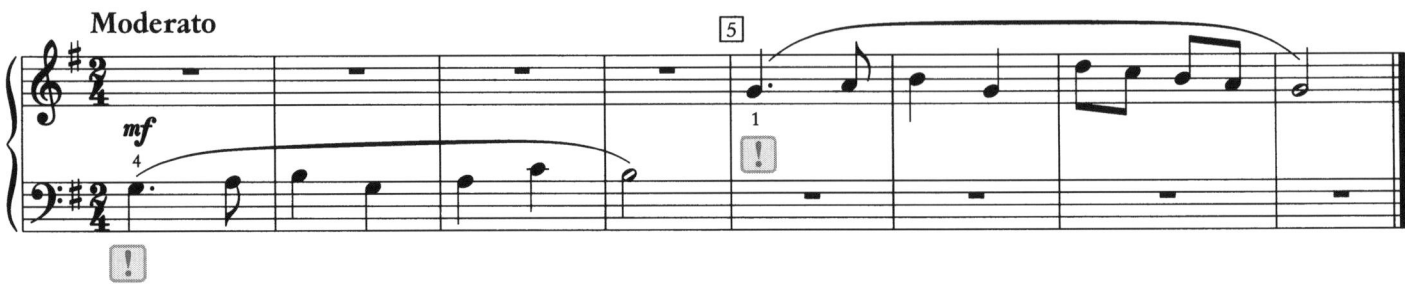

41

Do not forget to follow the **TRaK**, will you?

Be sure to give the dotted minims in bars 2 and 6 three steady counts.

? What is the value of the rest in bar 4 (left hand)?

Note how the melody moves mainly by step.

! **Watch out** for the dotted crotchet followed by the quaver in bar 7.

Play quite slowly this time.

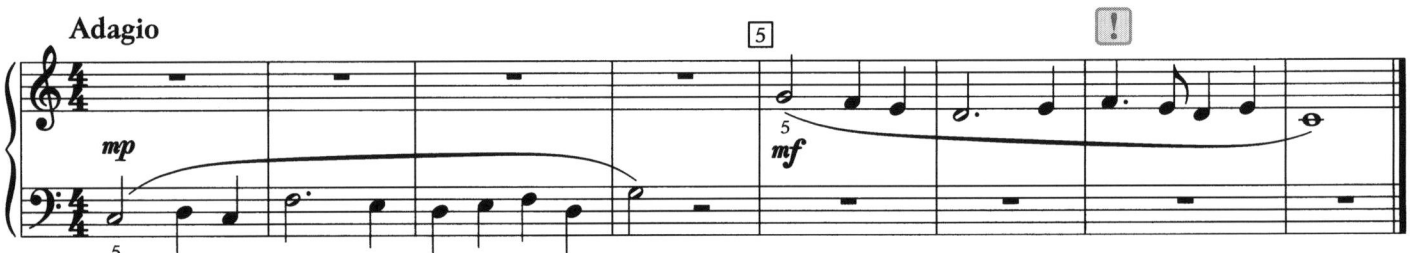

42

TRaK

? What is the value of the dot in a dotted crotchet?

Play the key-note, then the tonic chord.

The quavers in bars 5, 6 and 8 should be played very evenly.

Can you decide on the fingering?

What does *Tempo di valse* mean?

Observe the signs ⎯⎯⎯⎯ ⎯⎯⎯⎯.

! **Watch out** for the ♩. ♪ rhythm in bars 1, 3 and 7.

Remember to tap the rhythm a few times first then play with a good tone.

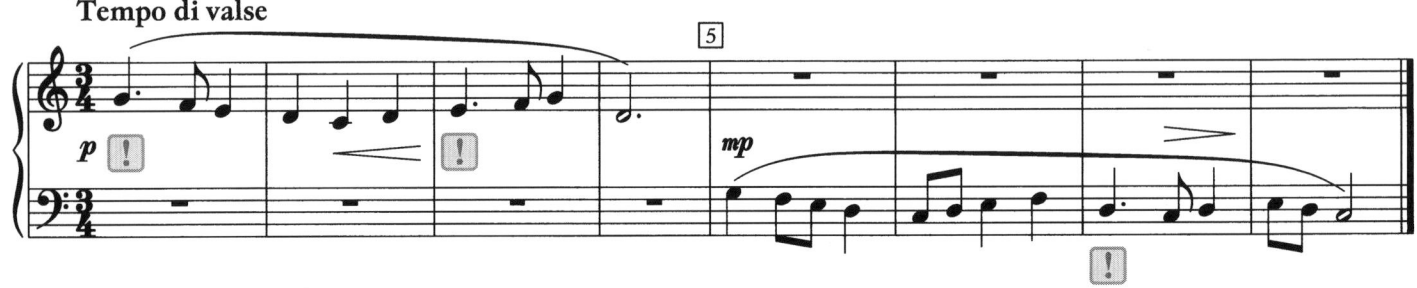

[T]ime, [R]hythm and [K]ey?
[?] How many intervals of a third are there?

Can you suggest a finger for the B minim in bar 5?

Do you notice the 'extra' phrase (or Coda) at the end of the piece?

[!] **Watch out** for the dotted crotchet followed by a quaver in bar 3.

See if there are any notes affected by the sharp.

Più means more: *più lento* means slower.
Play the coda **pp** (*pianissimo*).

43

Count as you play the piece through smoothly and remember, ... this is a dance.

[TRaK]

[?] Which is the best finger to use for the A in bar 9?

What is the meaning of > in bars 2, 4, 6 and 8?

The ♩. ♪ rhythm appears three times in this piece.

Note the coda at the end and have your 5th finger (right hand) ready to play.

Contrast the tone of the accents with crisp and light *staccato* playing.

44

Notice how the second half of this piece should be played more quietly and smoothly in contrast to the first section. The piece ends with more *staccato* notes in the right hand. Play with confidence.

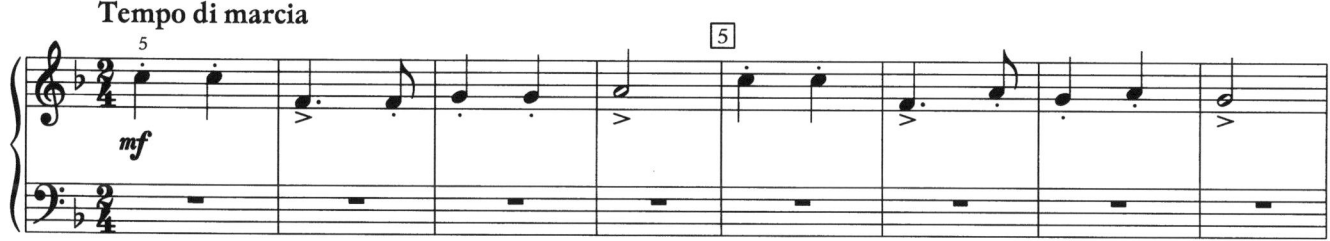

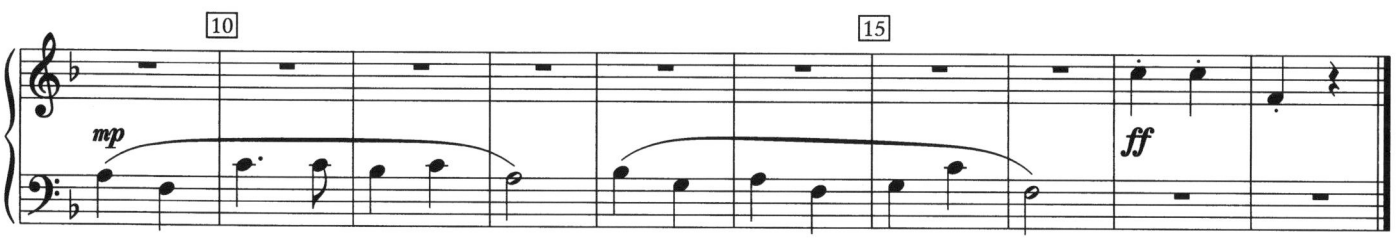

19

45

[TRaK] Time? Rhythm? and Key?

[?] What is the best fingering to use?

What is the meaning of *rit. e dim.*?

[!] **Watch out** for the ♩. ♪ rhythm in bars 1 and 3.

Find all the B♭s to be played.

Have your right hand ready to play again in bar 5.

Andante means play at a walking pace.

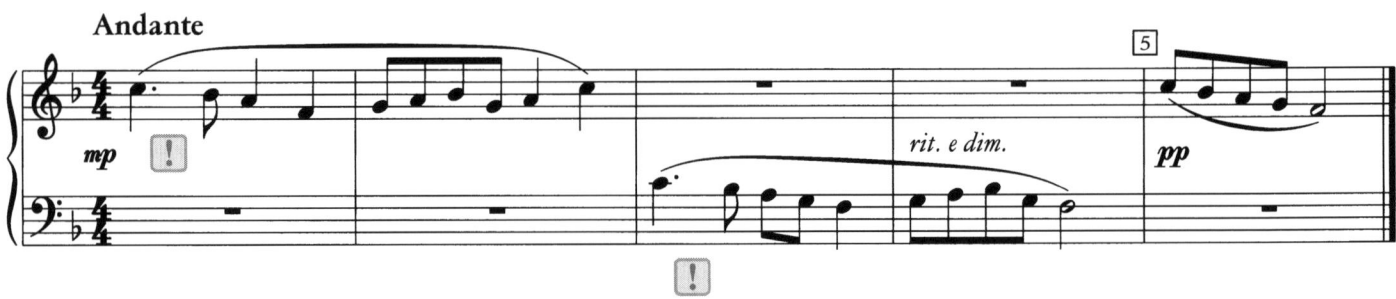

46

[TRaK]

[?] On which beat does the ♩. ♪ rhythm fall in bars 1, 3, 5 and 7?

What does *mp* mean?

What is the meaning of the sign ⟩ in bar 7?

[!] **Watch out** for the dotted crotchet followed by a quaver – it falls on the second beat.

Play the tonic chord.

This is in triple time and in the style of a waltz. Count carefully.

There is a **gradual** decrease in tone at the end.

This is a little more difficult and will need some practice. Clap the rhythm several times first before playing.

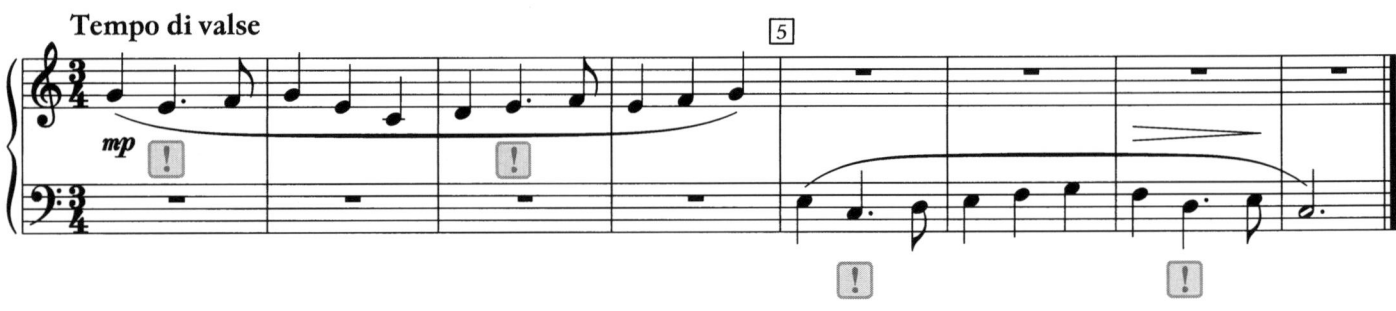

47

[T] Is this in duple or triple time?

[R] Can you note the ♩. ♪ rhythm falling on the second beat in bars 1 and 5?

[K] Which (major) key has a B♭ in the key signature?

[?] Can you plan the fingering?

State the value of each beat.

Tap this rhythm:

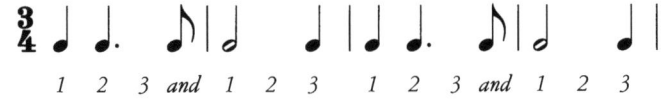

Place both hands on the keyboard.

Play very rhythmically.

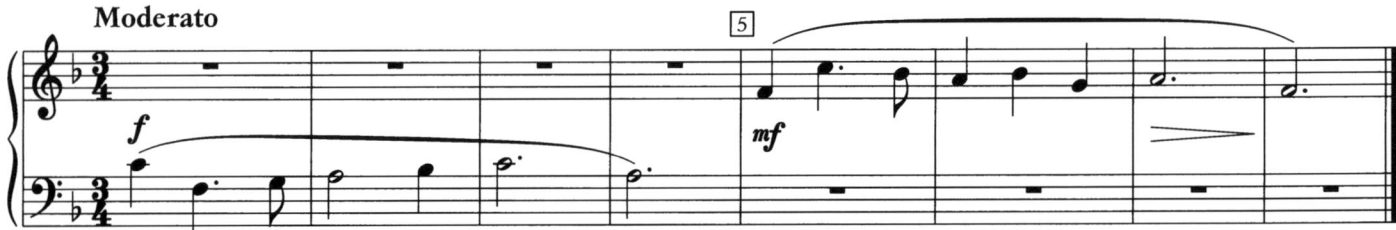

Introducing the key of D major and the time signatures of 2/2 and 3/8

T	What is waltz time?	The value of the beat is a	48
R	Can you tap the rhythm?	Count as you tap the rhythm.
K	How many sharps are there in the key signature?	Name the key. Find all the sharpened notes in the piece.
?	Can you plan the fingering?

Play gracefully. Now try and sing the melody in the treble clef, two bars at a time.

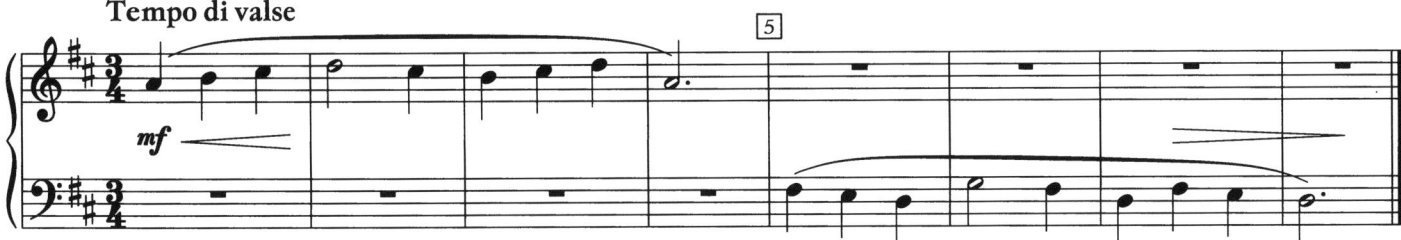

TRaK

? Which notes must be lowered one semitone?

Can you decide on the fingering for the first note in bar 5 (right hand)?

There are two **minim** beats in a bar.

Find two intervals of a fourth, one third and one fifth.

Place both hands over the keys before you begin so that the right hand is ready to play on time.

49

Play this peacefully (*tranquillo*) and smoothly (*legato*). Give the semibreves their full value.

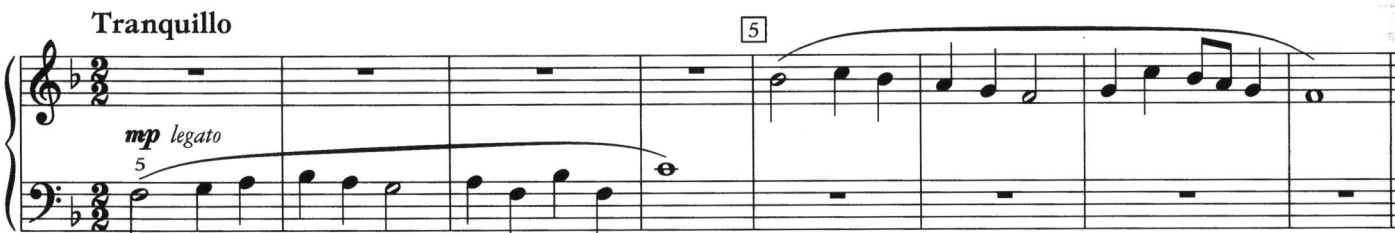

TRaK

? Is there a C that needs to be sharpened?

Which finger is best to use for the first note in bar 5?

Find all the sharps required. Name the key.

Notice the broken chord in bars 1 to 2.

Notice also the intervals in bars 5, 6 and 7.

50

Play firmly and loudly (*forte*) without your tone becoming harsh. Always look ahead.

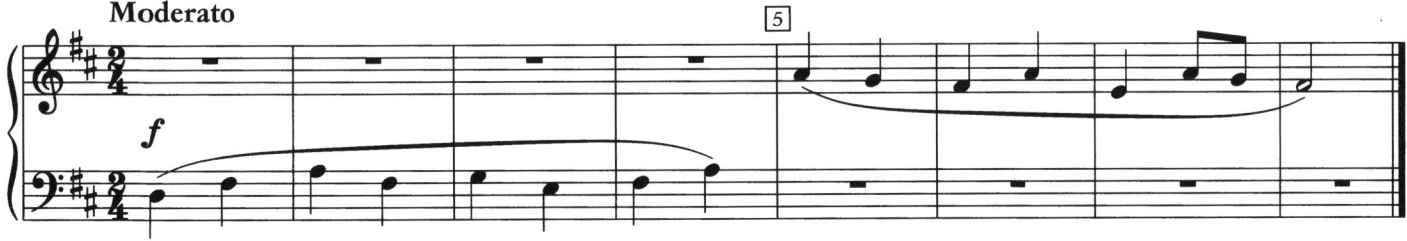

51 ⃞TRaK⃞   Remember to give the minims and dotted minims their full value.

⃞?⃞ Can you plan the fingering yourself?   Notice the pattern of the melody.

⃞!⃞ **Watch out** for the dotted crotchet followed by a quaver in bar 5.

Play gracefully.

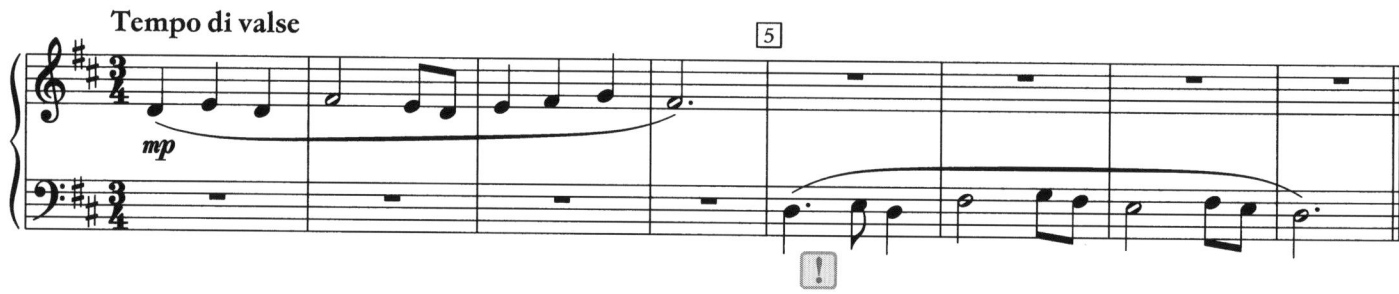

52 ⃞T⃞ How many beats are there in a bar?

⃞R⃞ Can you tap the rhythm?

⃞K⃞ How many sharps are there in the key signature?   Find all the notes affected by the sharps.

⃞?⃞ Which finger will you need to play the black keys?

Play straight through without stopping.

53 ⃞T⃞ How many beats are there in a bar?   The value of the beat is a **quaver**.

⃞R⃞ Can you tap the rhythm carefully?   Remember that in this piece there are two counts for the crotchets.

⃞K⃞ What is the key?

⃞!⃞ **Watch out** in bar 9 where the second beat is a crotchet.

This is a cheerful piece. Play the *staccato* notes crisply in contrast to the slurred notes.

Right@Sight

Introducing tied notes

TRaK   54

? Can you find the tied note?

What are the differences between bar 4 (left hand) and bar 5 (right hand)?

! **Watch out** for the crotchet rest in bar 5 (right hand).

This is a march. Remember to give all the crotchet rests their correct value.

Hold the tied note for its full value.

The extra ending to this piece is called a ....

The sign beneath the final C is an accent. Play this note strongly. Count steadily.

TRaK   55

? Which finger would you use for the A in bar 1?

What does f mean?

! **Watch out** for the tied notes in the first four bars. Make sure that these tied notes are held for the correct number of beats.

Clap **and count** the rhythm several times.

Do not forget to accent the notes marked > in bars 1 and 3 (right hand).

Maestoso means majestically.

The 'strong' beat in a bar is usually the first, but here the effect of the crotchet rest, together with the tied notes, is to make the accent fall on the weaker second beat of bars 1 and 3. The displacing of a strong beat to a weaker beat is known as **syncopation**. The accents marked below the A and B♭ reinforce the syncopation.

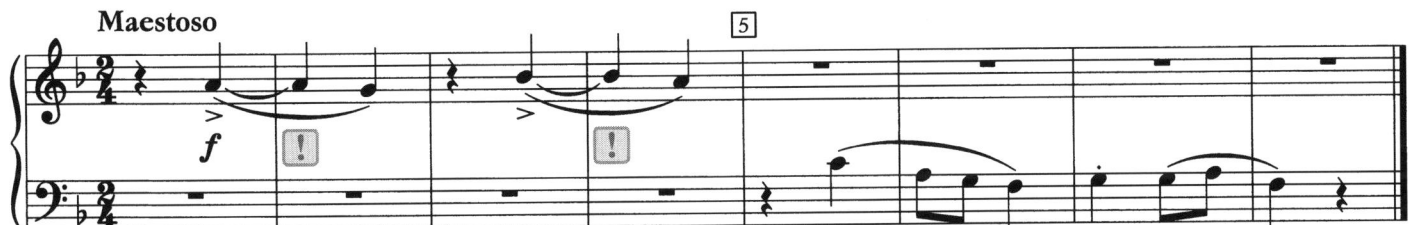

56

TRaK

[?] Are there any tied notes?

What is the meaning of **mp** and **pp**?

[!] **Watch out** for the *staccato* notes in bars 9 and 10 (right hand).

Observe the crotchet rests in bars 8, 9 and 10.

Notice the pattern of the melody and see how it moves in steps most of the time.

Play slowly (*Adagio*) without stopping, and make the music flow.

57

TRaK

[?] Is the time duple, triple or quadruple?

What is the meaning of **mp** and *legato*?

[!] **Watch out** for the crotchet rest and *staccato* note in the last bar.

There are tied notes in bars 1 to 2 (right hand) and bars 5 to 6 (left hand). Remember to hold these notes for their full value.

Play at a moderate pace. Do not look down at the keys.

58

TRaK

[?] What is the meaning of **p**, **f** and *dim.*?

[!] **Watch out** for the tied semibreve F and hold it while playing the notes above it in the right hand. Also look out for the two *staccato* notes in bar 7.

Find the tied notes.

The sign ⸺ means the same as *diminuendo*.

Remember to tap the rhythm. Then count as you play.

TRaK

[?] Can you find the tied notes and count them correctly?

What are the Italian terms for f and p ?

Play the tonic chord.

Hold the minims in the left hand while playing the notes above in the right hand.

59

Play through the piece in a quick and lively manner.
Play the right hand again, two bars at a time, and try to hum the melody as an echo.

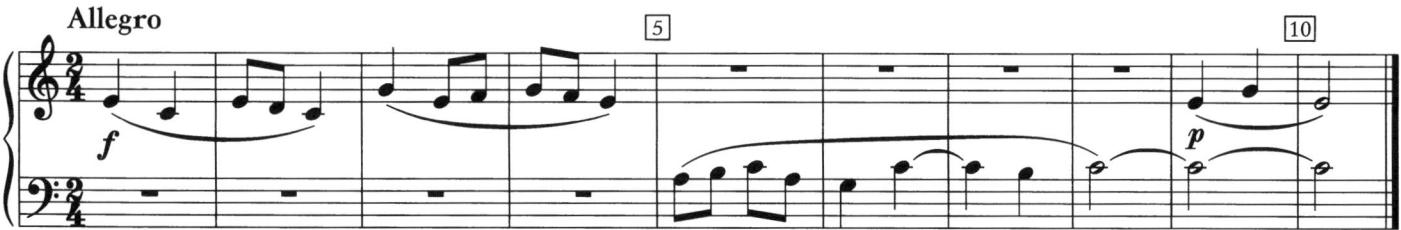

TRaK

[?] Can you find a tied note?

What is the meaning of mp?

What is the meaning of the *crescendo* and *diminuendo* signs?

[!] **Watch out** – do not confuse dotted crotchets with *staccato* notes.

Notice the dotted rhythm in bars 1 and 3.

Observe the rests in bars 5 and 7 (left hand).

The increase and decrease in the dynamics should be gradual.

60

Play this very gracefully.

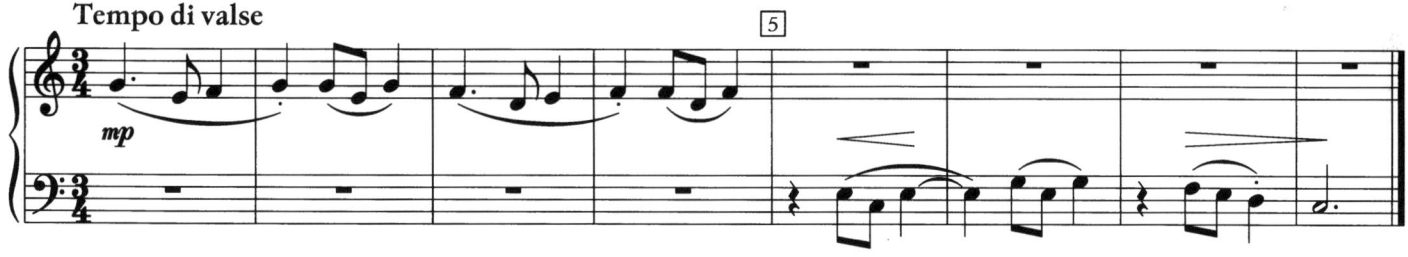

Follow the **TRaK**

[?] How many beats are to be held for the tied dotted minims in bars 8 to 10 (left hand)?

What is a coda?

Note the value of the dot in bar 1 and the dot in bar 3.

Remember to clap the rhythm.

Note the *ritenuto* in the final bars.

61

Play the piece very lightly.

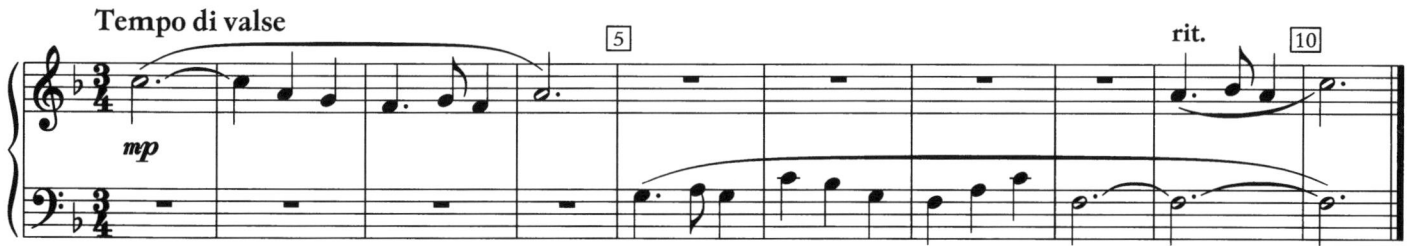

62	T How many beats are there in a bar?	The value of the beat is a quaver.
	R Can you tap the rhythm carefully?	Observe all the tied notes.
	K What is the key?	Find all the notes affected by the flat in the key signature.
	! **Watch out** for the quaver rest in bar 11.	

Play cheerfully. Look ahead.

63	TRaK	Note the two sharps in the key signature.
	? Can you find any tied notes?	Hold the tied notes for their full value.
	What does *ben marcato* mean?	

Play this piece purposefully, observing the phrasing.

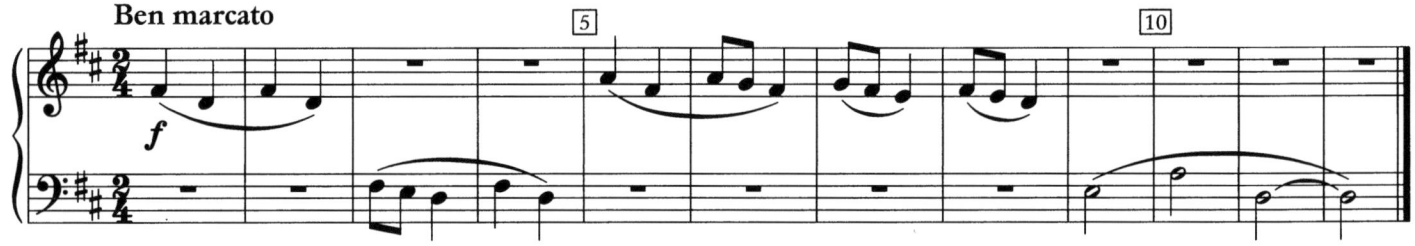

64	Follow the TRaK	There are .... beats in a bar.
	? Can you find the tied notes?	Hold the tied notes for their full value.
	Can you plan the fingering?	Have your fingers ready over the black keys in bars 1 and 5.
	! **Watch out** for the timing in bar 4 (right hand).	

Play through steadily and quietly.

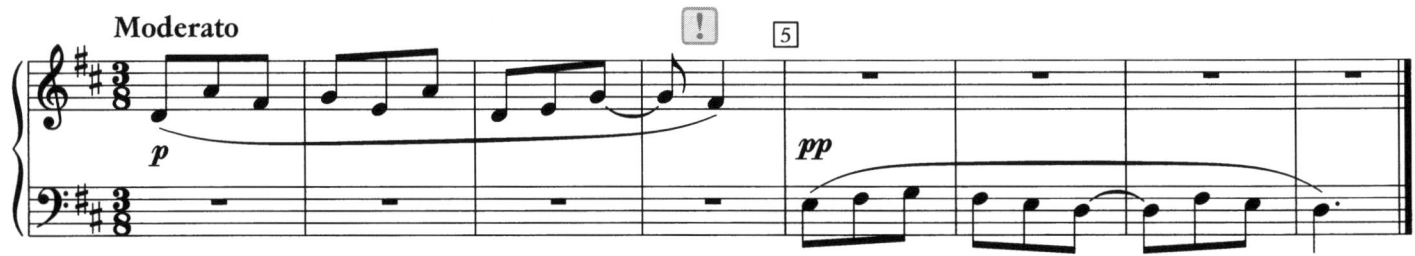

Right@Sight

Introducing accidentals, and the keys of A minor and D minor

TRaK

K Is this key major or minor?

? Can you see the small scale passage in the left hand?

! **Watch out** for the interval of a third in bar 7 (left hand).

Count and clap the rhythm carefully.

Name the accidental in bar 3.
This is the sharpened seventh note of the scale.

65

Make sure that the correct fingers are placed over the black notes before you begin to play.
This melody has a rather sad mood.

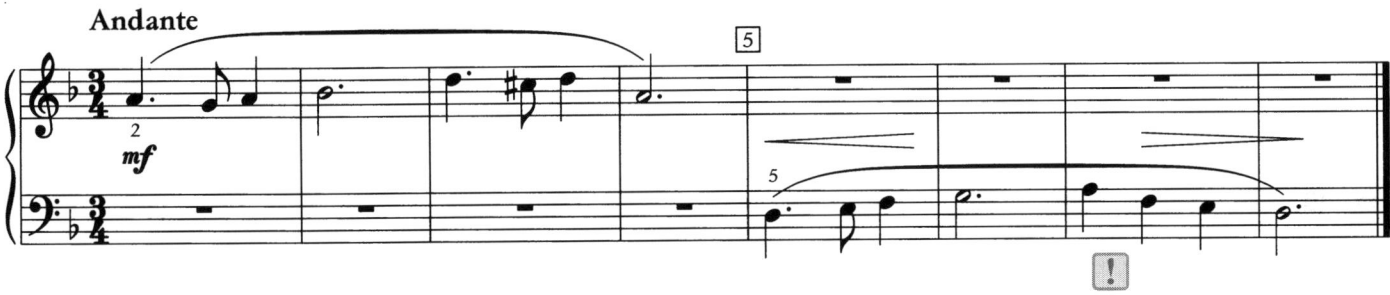

Follow the **TRaK**

? How many accidentals can you find?

Are there any tied notes?

Can you observe the fingering marked in bars 3, 4 and 7?

Hold the minims and dotted minims for their correct value.

66

Play the piece with a light tone. Keep your eyes looking ahead to the next bar.

67

[T] What is the value of each beat? | This time is called *Alla breve*.

[R] Can you tap the rhythm accurately first time? | Keep counting. Give the minims and semibreves their proper value.

[K] Is the key major or minor? | Look at the accidentals before deciding on the key. Also look at the key-note or tonic in bar 8.

[?] Which note is always raised a semitone in the harmonic minor scale? Which finger should you use for the A in bar 1 (right hand)?

[!] **Watch out** for the tied notes.

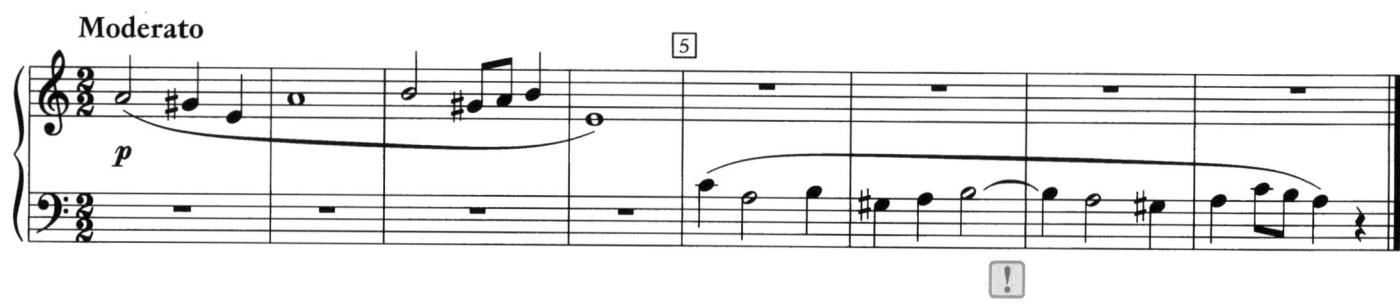

68

[TRaK] | Notice that in bar 3 the B♭ is raised a semitone by a natural sign. Find all the accidentals.

[?] What do you notice about the melody in bars 1 and 2?

[!] Watch out in bar 2 (right hand) where the thumb turns under the second finger (having played F♯ in bar 1), in order to play the G on the first beat of bar 2. The thumb should do the work here, not the elbow!

Play expressively (*espressivo*).

69

[TRaK] What is the value of each beat? | There are .... beats in a bar.

[?] Are there both F♯s and C♯s in the melody? | Also check to see if there are any accidentals.

Make sure that all the quavers are evenly timed and neatly joined.

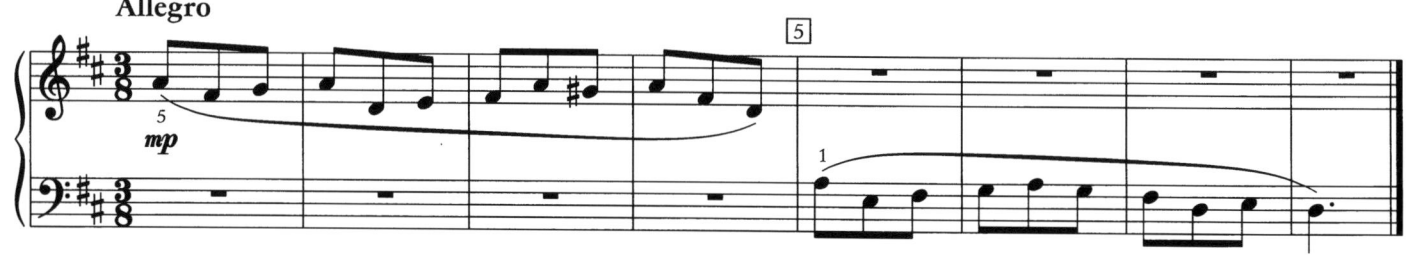

Look at the TRaK

[?] Can you find all the accidentals?

What does **f** mean?

[!] **Watch out** for the change of fingering on the repeated notes. This helps to prevent a harsh tone.

Observe the crotchet rests.

Remember, an accidental lasts until the end of the bar.

Staccato notes in bars 1, 2 and 5 need to be very crisp.

70

Play confidently.

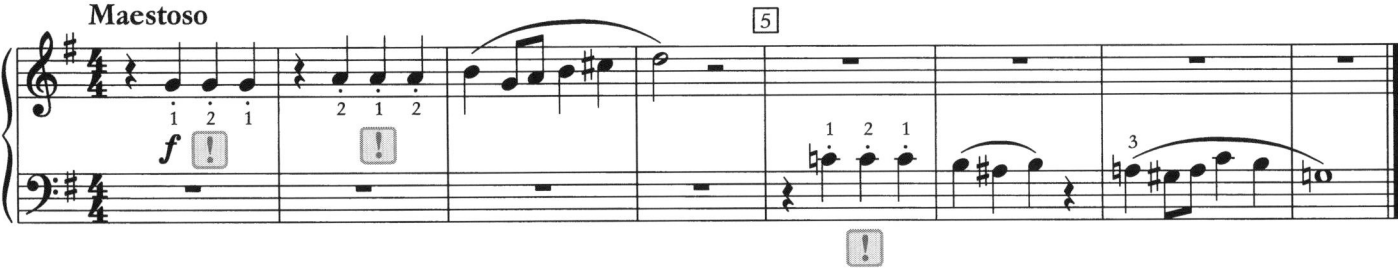

TRaK

[?] Are there any tied notes?

[!] **Watch out** – a change of hand position is needed to play bars 9 and 10 (right hand). Practise moving the right hand from one position to the other (from bar 6 to bar 9).

The key is minor. If you cannot name it, look at the G♯s and at the tonic or key-note in the last bar.

Remember what *rit. e dim.* means.

71

Play rather sadly.

Follow the TRaK

[?] How many accidentals are there?

Can you plan the fingering carefully before you begin?

[!] **Watch out** for the ledger line in the last bar.

The value of the beat is a ……………………… .

Remember the flat in the key signature when you play bar 5.

72

Make the music flow.

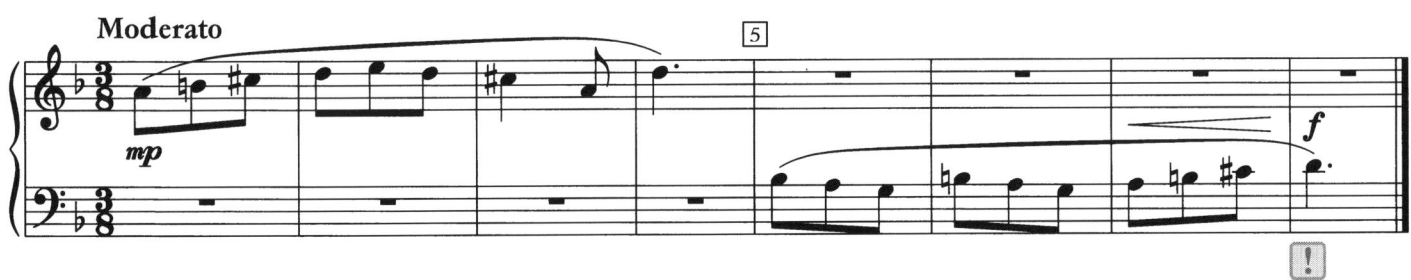

73

- **T** What is the time signature?
- **R** Can you tap the rhythm carefully?
- **K** Can you name the key? — Name the minor scale which has F# and G# in the ascending form, and G♮ and F♮ in the descending form.
- **?** Can you find the tied notes? — Hold the tied notes for the correct number of beats in the last few bars.
- **!** **Watch out** for the change in hand position that is required for the coda in bar 9 (left hand). Practise moving the left hand from the position in bars 3 and 4 to the new position in bar 9.

Play *pianissimo*.

74

TRaK   Find the accidental.

! **Watch out** for the timing in bars 2 and 4. Count carefully and bring in the right hand quavers (bar 2) and the left hand crotchet (bar 4) at precisely the correct time.

Remember to tap first. Then play very rhythmically and strongly.

75

As usual, follow the **TRaK**   The timing of the quaver rests needs special care.

Note the little scale passage in bar 6.

! **Watch out** for the repeated notes in bars 1, 3 and 5: time them very evenly and play with a crisp *staccato* touch.

For extra practice in fingering, you might like to suggest a change of fingers for each of the repeated notes.

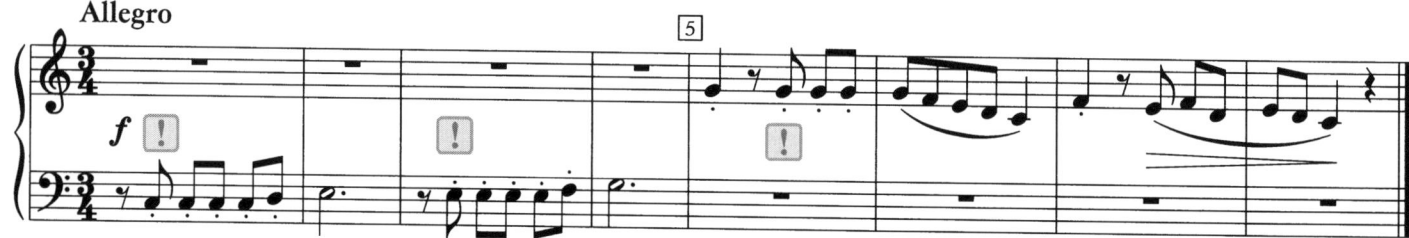

Right@Sight

On your own now ...

The following pieces do not have hints to help.

Remember... follow the TRaK, look ahead, keep counting and keep going!

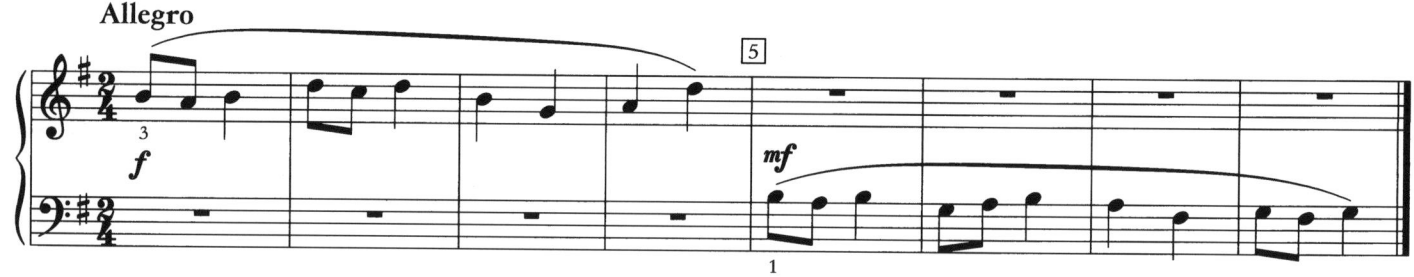
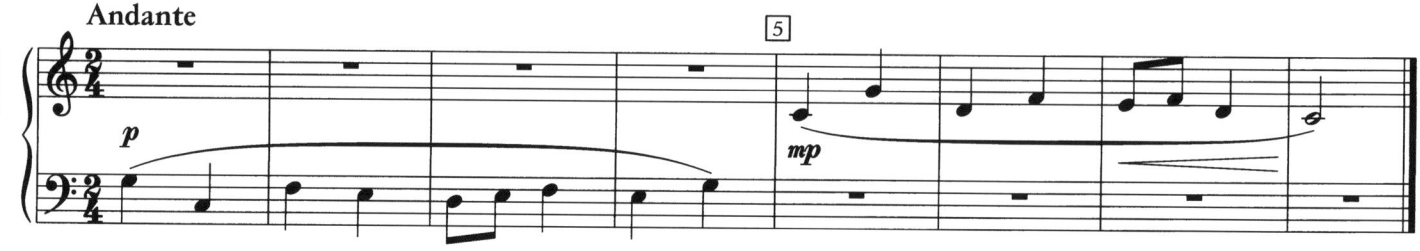

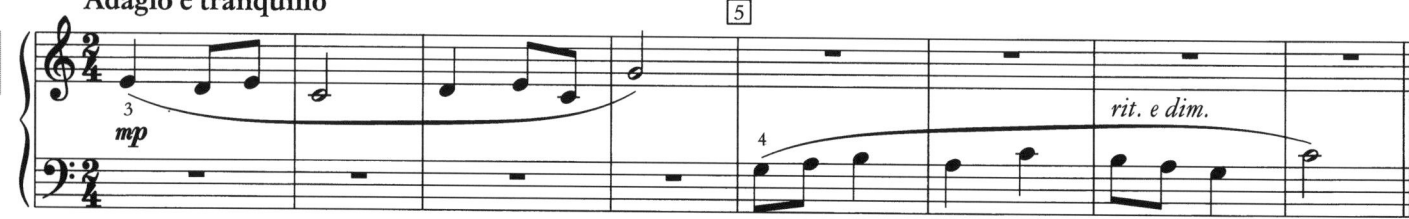

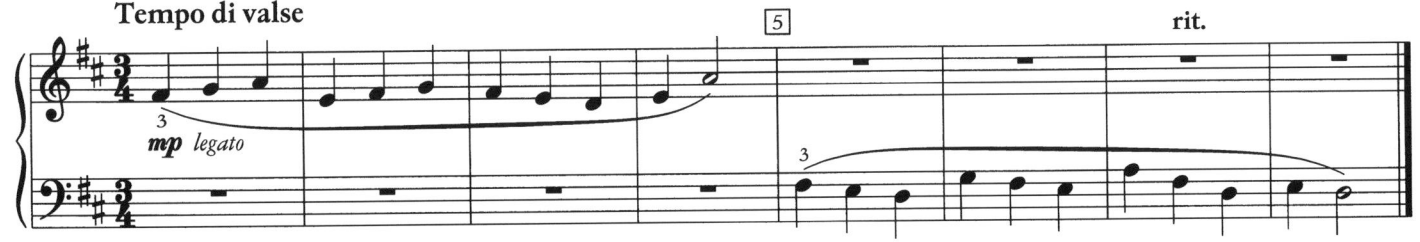
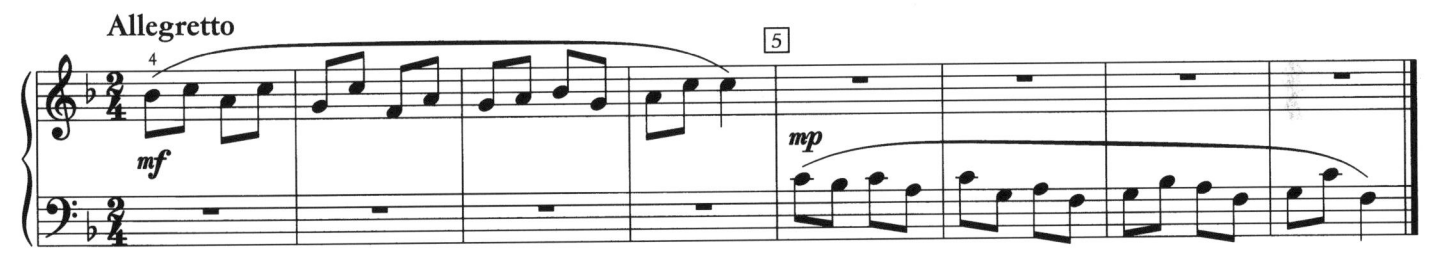

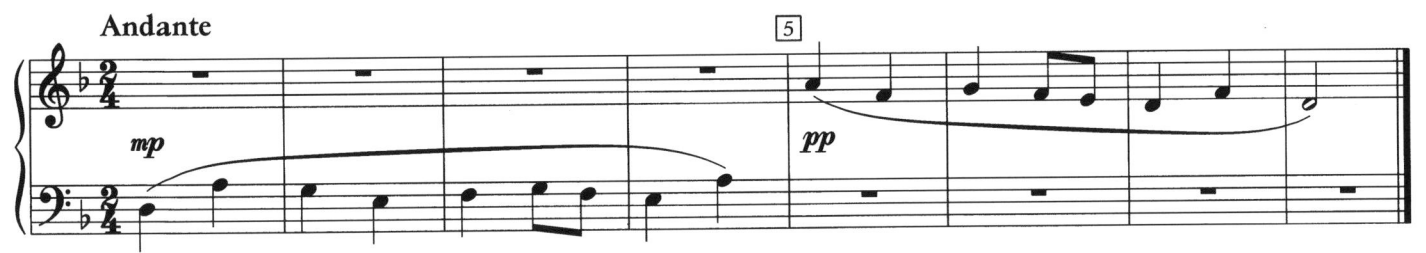
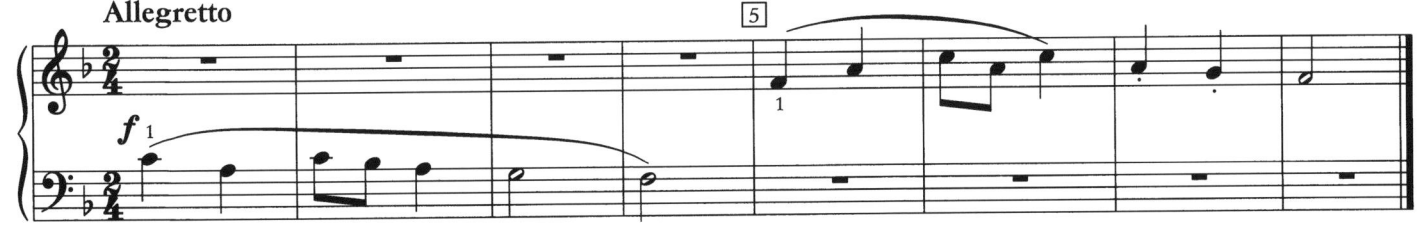

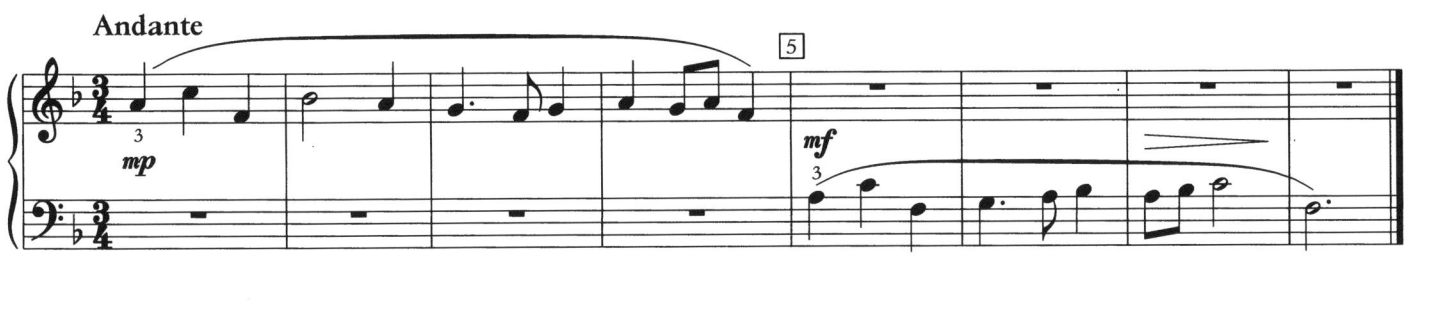
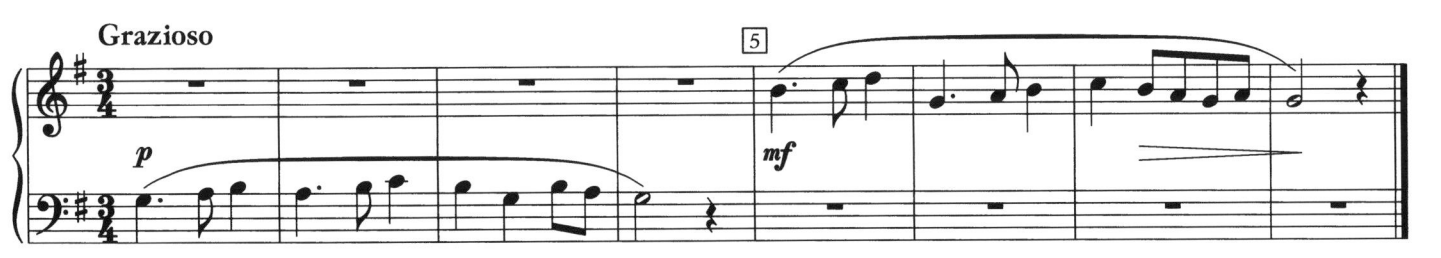
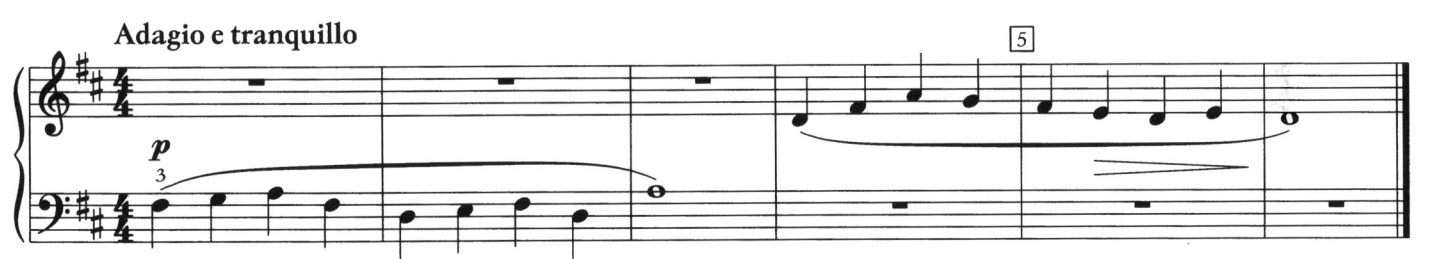
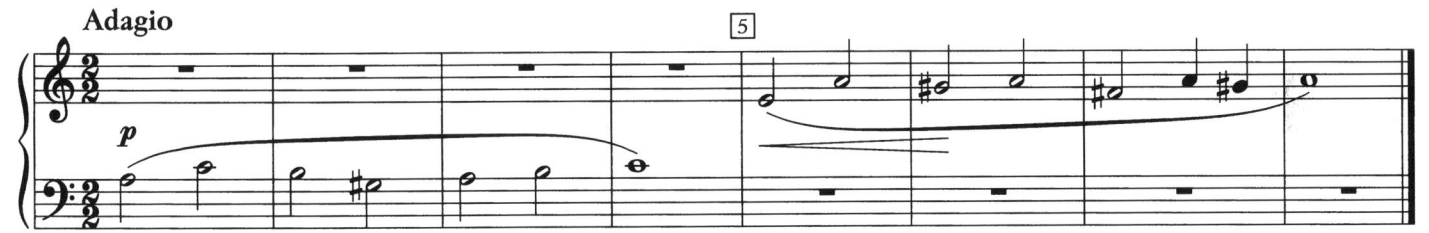
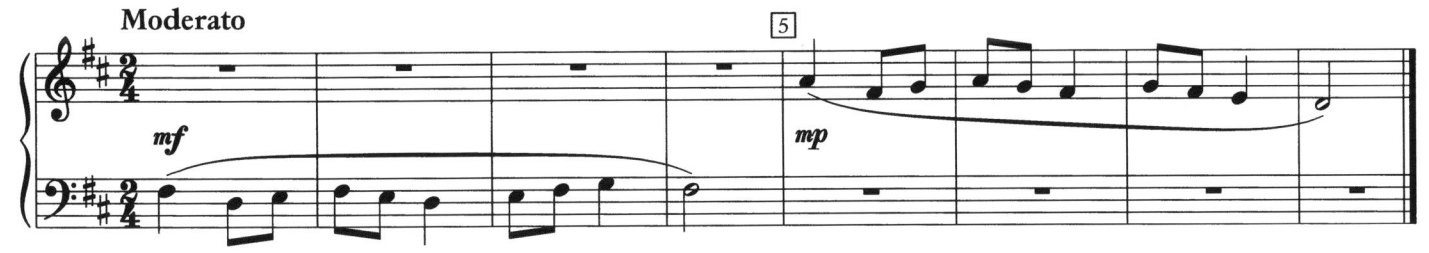
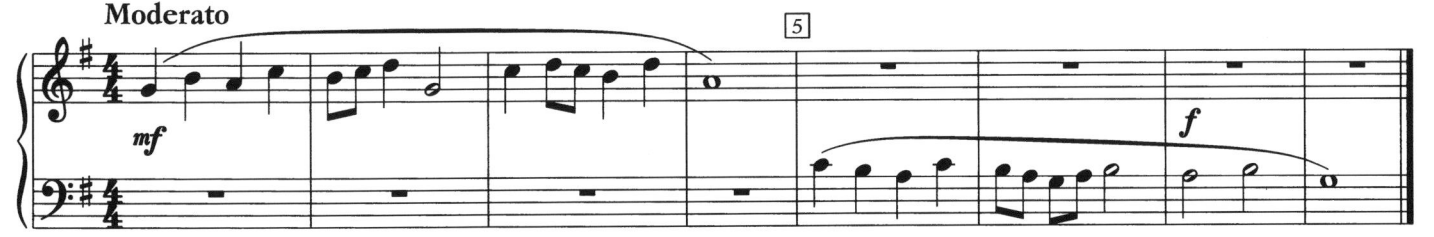

36

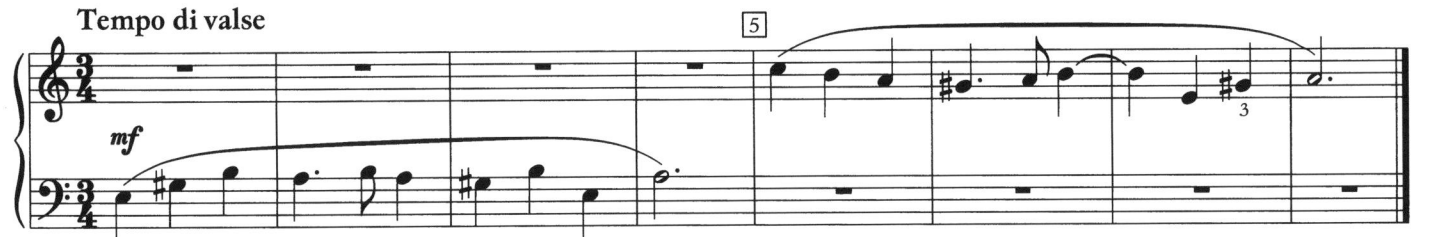

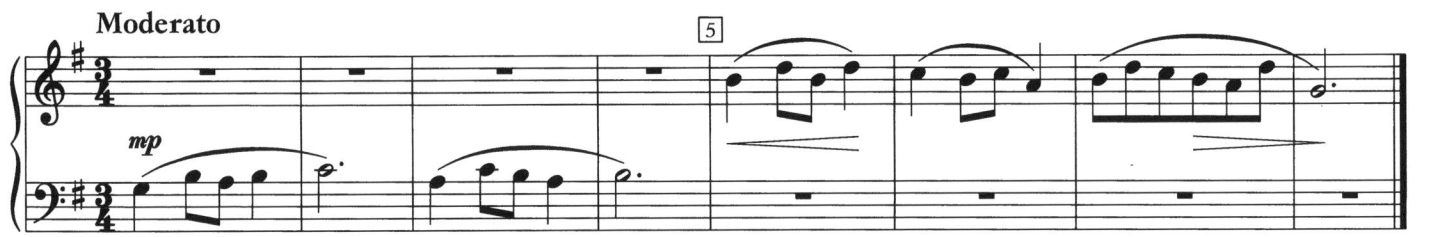

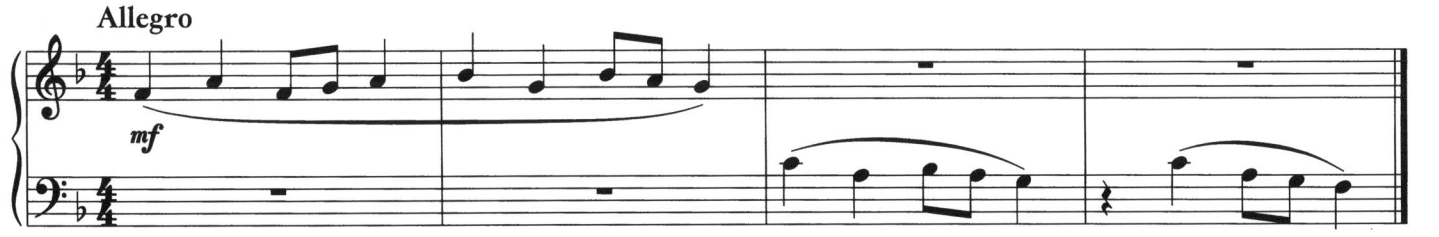

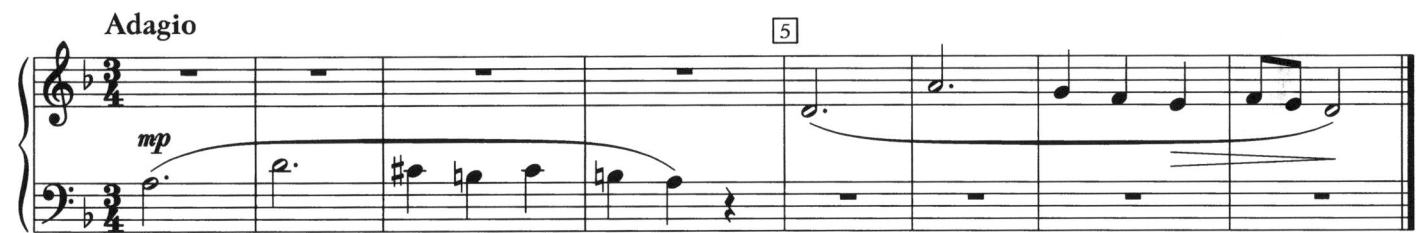

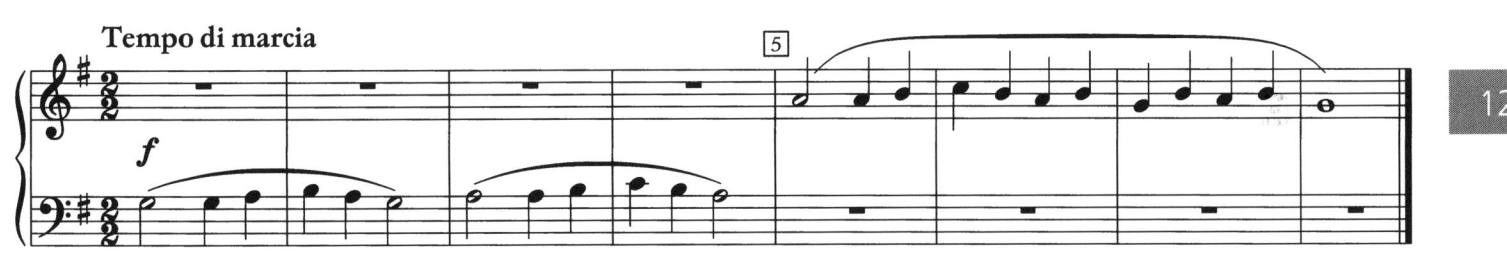

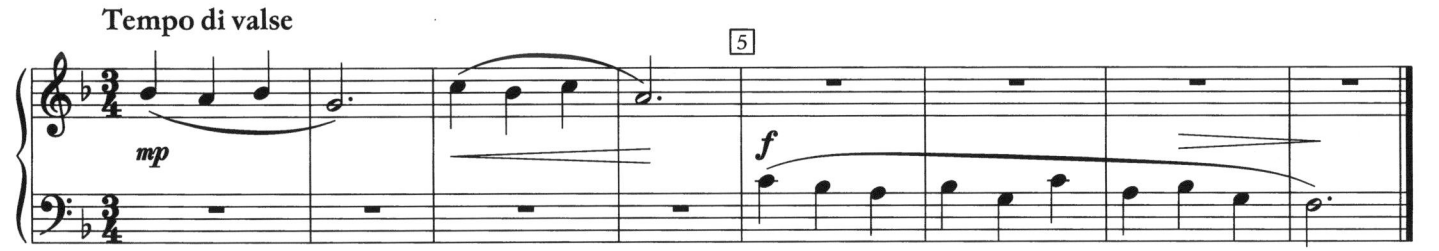

Glossary of musical terms and symbols

Adagio	Slowly
Alla breve	2/2 – two minim beats in a bar
Alla marcia	In the style of a march
Allegretto	Fairly quick, not as fast as *Allegro*
Allegro	(*lit.* cheerful) Quick, lively
Andante	Walking pace; moderate speed
Ben marcato	Very accented
Coda	(*lit.* a tail) A small passage added to the end of a piece
Con moto	With movement
Crescendo, cresc.	Gradually becoming louder
Diminuendo, dim.	Gradually becoming quieter
Espressivo	Expressive
Forte, **f**	Loud
Fortissimo, **ff**	Very loud
Grazioso	Graceful
Largo	Slow and stately
Legato	Smooth
Maestoso	Majestic
Mezzo forte, **mf**	Moderately loud
Mezzo piano, **mp**	Moderately quiet
Moderato	Moderate speed
Piano, **p**	Quiet
Pianissimo, **pp**	Very quiet
Più lento	Slower (*più*: more)
Ritenuto, rit.	Held back
Staccato, stacc.	Detached
Tempo di marcia	In the time (and style) of a march
Tempo di menuetto	In the time (and style) of a minuet
Tempo di valse	In the time (and style) of a waltz
Tranquillo	Calm and tranquil
Vivace	Lively, quick
$<$	Gradually becoming louder
$>$	Gradually becoming quieter
>	Accent